HOW TO BE
A SUCCESSFUL
LIFE COACH

If you want to know how...

Learning to Counsel
Develop the skills, insight and knowledge to counsel others

Learning to Coach
For personal and professional development

Free Yourself from Anxiety
A self-help guide to overcoming anxiety disorders

365 Ways to be Your Own Life Coach

365 Steps to Self-Confidence

howtobooks

Send for a free copy of the latest catalogue to:

How To Books
Spring Hill House, Spring Hill Road, Begbroke
Oxford OX5 1RX. United Kingdom.
email: info@howtobooks.co.uk
www.howtobooks.co.uk

HOW TO BE A SUCCESSFUL LIFE COACH

A GUIDE TO SETTING UP A PROFITABLE COACHING BUSINESS

Shelagh Young

howtobooks

Published by How To Books Ltd,
Spring Hill House, Spring Hill Road,
Begbroke, Oxford OX5 1RX. United Kingdom.
Tel: (01865) 375794. Fax: (01865) 379162.
info@howtobooks.co.uk
www.howtobooks.co.uk

How To Books greatly reduce the carbon footprint of their books by sourcing their typesetting and printing in the UK.

British Library Cataloguing in Publication Data
A catalogue record for this book is available from the British Library

ISBN 978 1 84528 296 7

Cover design by Baseline Arts Ltd, Oxford
Produced for How To Books by Deer Park Productions, Tavistock, Devon
Typeset by PDQ Typesetting, Newcastle-under-Lyme, Staffs.
Printed and bound by Bell & Bain Ltd, Glasgow

NOTE: The material contained in this book is set out in good faith for general guidance and no liability can be accepted for loss or expense incurred as a result of relying in particular circumstances on statements made in the book. Laws and regulations are complex and liable to change, and readers should check the current position with the relevant authorities before making personal arrangements.

Contents

What is Coaching?

If you have already studied to become a coach you already know the answer to this question. If you think you know exactly what coaching is then you can afford to skip a few pages to Chapter 2 and start thinking about how to develop your coaching skills to the point at which you can run a successful coaching business. If you have any doubts whatsoever then read on. Knowing exactly what we mean by 'coaching' is not always as simple as it seems.

At the most basic level coaching is a conversation. Only it isn't the kind of conversation most of us would want to have with our friends when we are out to have fun. For a start, an effective coaching session should be hard work for both the coach and their client. The client has to do a lot of thinking and talking. The coach has to do a lot of thinking and listening. Both have to be 100 per cent focused on the coaching session and 100 per cent committed to bringing it to a successful conclusion. If they are not, then the session will not deliver the best possible results.

None of this is captured by the dictionary definition of coaching. Almost anyone with adequate knowledge of a subject can do what the *Concise Oxford Dictionary* defines as coaching, which is to:

tutor, train, give hints to, prime with facts

This definition barely skims the surface of what you will do in your new business. To be successful in coaching you will need to build a good quality relationship with every client. This is because coaching works by encouraging and enabling the client to take responsibility for their learning and achievements. There is very little teaching involved in a coaching. The process of coaching is designed to help people to learn by drawing on their own resources and resources they set out to find. It is not about spoon-feeding clients with facts or a great deal of information. This is why conversations which form the basis of all coaching work must be quite one-sided. It is the coach's job to listen and reflect back key points to the client in order to help them focus on how they will bring about change. A coach who says too much is unlikely to be meeting the client's needs.

Coaching is still not widely understood. Most of us want information and advice to help us change our lives. Lots of your clients will try to extract information and advice from you. Don't let them succeed. You are not an expert advisor. You are a coach. If your prospective clients do not understand what it is that you have to offer then make sure you have a short, clear way of letting them know.

CREATING YOUR 'ELEVATOR PITCH'

Take a moment to think about what you will say when someone asks you what you do or what working with a coach will be like. In the film and television business people talk about having an elevator pitch ready. An elevator pitch is just a short, sharp, motivating and engaging summary of their TV or film idea. It is for those moments, such as when you share a lift, when you meet someone you want to influence. You can't risk boring them and they are too busy to make an appointment to see you. So you briskly pitch your idea whenever you get the chance. A successful coach needs to be able to do this too.

What will your elevator pitch be? Try writing down some options. Then say them out loud. Do they roll off the tongue easily? Try them out with an honest friend or family member. Do they get your meaning? Are they excited by the idea of coaching? The opportunity to pitch for coaching business is there every time someone asks you what you do, so your first attempt should work as an answer to the typical question: 'What do you do?'

My elevator pitch

I'm a coach actually.

I...

....

....

....

....

....

Here's my card. Call me when I can help you.

This elevator pitch is really important because an excellent coach leads a process that differs quite a lot from the general common sense understanding of what coaching entails. This is possibly because the first ideas that come to mind when most of us think about 'coaching' are examples from sport. The sports coach is the most well-known example of a coach in action. When we think about sports and what a team or individual sports coach does we often imagine someone who tells the athletes or players what to do and how to do it. For example, explaining or demonstrating better techniques for running, instructing in the art of the successful tackle or telling athletes what to eat to stay in peak fitness.

We can visualise the coach shouting advice from the sidelines or holding a stopwatch and timing training runs. The coach will probably pat the sportsperson on the back when they have done well and give them a pep talk when they haven't achieved a hoped-for result or a personal best. We don't tend to imagine the athlete saying much when the coach is on the scene. In this scenario we invest the coach with the expertise, knowledge, solutions and authority and the athletes just do what is asked of them.

Luckily, this is not how the best sports coaches work and it is certainly not the best way for you to help anyone achieve their personal best. Of course it is possible to assist people to learn new technical skills by showing and telling. For example, an athlete aiming to win a hurdles race will need to learn the best-known way of running such a race. However, the limitations of this approach have been proved time and again. In high jump competitions everyone used to jump by running and executing a scissors-style jump which straddled the bar. They were jumping as they had been told to do. Now nobody jumps this way because someone came up with a better idea.

In 1968, Dick Fosbury decided to try a different style of jump which he believed would enable him to clear greater heights. Dick Fosbury invented the Fosbury Flop, a technically more efficient means of jumping which enables athletes to use their body weight to help their feet clear the bar. Presumably it took quite a lot of guts to run up to a bar and throw himself over it backwards when everyone was doing it differently (especially before special padded landing areas were introduced once his idea caught on), and this is exactly why coaching is also about supporting clients. Our clients are often trying to do something new, different and challenging. Everyone needs support when they decide to push themselves to achieve more or achieve things differently. Trying new things isn't easy, and even with the laws of physics on his side Dick Fosbury probably had his moments of doubt. The point is he wanted to jump higher. This was his goal and he worked out a means by which he felt he could achieve that goal.

HELPING PEOPLE FIND OUT WHAT THEY WANT TO DO

Helping people find out what they want to do and how they are going to do it is the essence of coaching. So if someone asks you what you do as a coach try telling them this: 'I help you find out what you really want to do. Then I help you work out how you will do it and when.'

The 'when' is the golden key in coaching. It is only when the majority of your coaching sessions end with your clients knowing what they want, what they will do to get it, how they will do it and when they will do it, that you can ever really claim to be coaching successfully. And never forget that real success is defined by goals achieved. Good intentions are the starting point not the end point of effective coaching.

TOP FOUR COACHING RULES

Coaching successfully is a thrilling, engaging occupation. It is also highly challenging because so much of the success of every coaching session depends on you. You cannot achieve goals for your client but by abiding by some clear coaching principles you can ensure that you maximise your client's ability to set and achieve ambitious goals as a result of your coaching. For your coaching to be successful you must be working with a client who has the will to make change happen. Your job is to inspire them and help them find the motivation to take the first step and follow through to the end.

There are four key principles which must always inform your behaviour as a coach. As a coach you should always:

1   Build your coaching relationships on the basis of honesty, openness and trust.

2   Accept that your client is responsible for the results they achieve.

3   Always focus on the client.

4   Always believe in your client's ability to achieve more and better results.

The skilled coach makes putting these principles into action look easy but it is challenging work. If you hold to these four principles you will create a sound basis for effective coaching.

RELATIONSHIP BUILDING

When your clients trust you enough to open up and begin to

share their innermost thoughts, their dreams and their nightmares you have the raw material for making your coaching work effectively. Clients will always open up to you if they firmly believe that you are listening to them and have their best interests at heart. The trick is to make this happen quickly. Clients want to feel they are moving forward. You do not have the luxury of lengthy sessions for building trust. Clients want progress from the very first session. And why not?

So, you can build relationships quickly by sticking to the very basics of coaching.

- Never dominate the coaching conversation. Let your clients do most of the talking at every stage of your interaction. This is where your elevator pitch comes in handy too. You need to explain what you do very quickly to allow space for clients to talk.

- Don't play the expert. It is often useful if you 'give hints' and coaches may well 'prime with facts', as suggested by the dictionary definition of coaching. However, it is not your job to dominate the conversation or assume the expert role in the relationship.

- Show quickly that you trust your clients to find the best solutions for them. Trusting your client includes trusting them to set their own challenges and find their own solutions. Start by responding to their concerns with a phrase that lets them know you believe in their ability to make changes happen. Sounds hard? Look at the examples in the box. How hard can it be to come up with your own phrases along these lines?

> 'You probably know what would be best in this situation. Tell me what you've been thinking so far.'
>
> 'It sounds as if you know what to do. Tell me what you want to do next.'
>
> 'You've obviously thought about this a lot. What would make it easier to reach a decision?'
>
> 'I'm impressed by your insights. When will you make a decision?'
>
> 'You've obviously worked hard on developing these skills/ideas/ options. Tell me what your next step will be.'

Every time you show you trust your client you will boost their confidence. Confident people find it a whole lot easier to place their trust in others.

Remember, the importance of trust in the coaching relationship applies to every party. If you do not trust a client, particularly when this lack of trust takes the form of doubting the client's ability to succeed in their chosen field, you should not work with that client. Coaching is based on the belief that goals are most likely to be achieved when the clients set them for themselves and work out their own ways of achieving them. If you are cynical about a client's ability you have no useful role to play in this process and almost certainly risk undermining your client.

You will limit your client's achievements if you hold limiting beliefs about them and their abilities. However good you are at covering your true feeling they are likely to leak out during your contact with a client and have a negative impact on your client. If you do not believe in your client's ability then your client will pick up negative signals from you either consciously or unconsciously. This will undermine trust. A client who does not trust you is unlikely to achieve their full potential with you as their coach.

What are limiting beliefs?

A limiting belief is an untested idea about yourself which prevents you from taking certain actions or believing in certain possibilities.

If you believe you cannot learn to drive you are unlikely to take lessons. If you take a driving lesson and do not do very well you have not tested your belief. To test the belief you would have to stick at driving lessons for quite some time. You would need some objective proof of your assumed inability.

If you believe you are too ugly to find a lover you might think you have proved the fact because you don't have a special person in your life. What you have probably proved is that people who don't socialise a lot, ask people out or try Internet and other dating services have fewer dates, fewer lovers and fewer successful sexual relationships than people who do all these things.

Limiting beliefs stop you from making changes in your life because you don't see the point. They:

- undermine confidence
- stop you from acting to change your situation
- make you unhappy
- affect the way other people relate to you
- keep a vicious circle going in which not trying leads to not succeeding which is interpreted, wrongly, as objective proof of inability.

Coaching is about removing limiting beliefs and keeping the client convinced of his/her ability to make positive change happen.

WHAT COACHING IS NOT

- Coaching is not therapy.
- Coaching is not counselling.
- Coaching is not advice-giving.

Many people would describe their experience of being coached as highly therapeutic. What they might mean by this is that the coaching has helped them to satisfactorily address what they perceive to be problems in their lives. They might mean that coaching has helped them to feel happier or less stressed. They might even mean that coaching has led them to feel healthier and more energised than they felt at the start of the coaching process.

All of these things can fall from coaching. There is absolutely no doubt that coaching can help improve a person's physical and mental well-being. BUT COACHING IS NOT A FORM OF THERAPY.

Understanding the difference between coaching and counselling

So what's the difference between coaching and counselling or other forms of therapeutic intervention? Some counsellors would argue that the difference between coaching and some forms of therapy and counselling is too slight to be defined. Some coaches would also say that there are so many different forms of counselling and therapy, and that some resemble coaching so closely that it is meaningless to try to define the 'difference' between them.

There is no real need to strive to define the difference between coaching and counselling and therapy, but it is really helpful if you remain clear about what coaching is and what it entails. Coaching makes demands on your clients and you have to work only with those clients who are sufficiently robust to respond to those demands. You cannot tailor your coaching to make it more like counselling. It is what it is and should not be watered down when you suspect a client is not coping with life very well. Use your listening skills to work out what is going on for a client and help them set goals they can achieve at this stage of their lives.

Coaching and mental health

It would be absolutely wrong to insist that anyone with any form of mental illness was unsuited to coaching either as a coach or a client. Depression is a mental illness, a very common one which most people experience at least once in their lives. At the same time it is unfair to engage with a client who you believe to be too vulnerable or distressed to benefit from coaching and unethical to pretend that coaching is an adequate means of addressing serious mental ill health.

You should NEVER work with clients who manifest obvious signs of serious mental ill health without ensuring they are being adequately supported and/or treated by others. Even if you suspect that a very mild form of depression might be leading your client to be unhappy or to fail to achieve goals, you should encourage them to seek appropriate professional help. You should give serious consideration to suspending your coaching until they are feeling better or getting the additional help they need elsewhere.

There is more information on this important topic in Chapter 10.

WHAT COACHING ENTAILS

Before starting work with any client you should be clear about the following.

■ **Coaching focuses on results and outcomes**
The coaching session might be described by the client as having cheered them up or made them feel better but the session is never an end in itself. Every session should result in goals having been set by the client.

■ **Coaching focuses on the future**
The client might want to explore why they behave as they do but the coach should always push for action rather than diagnosis. The objective of every session is to move through reflection (if this is useful for the client) and towards action. Coaching is about what a client will do rather than why they haven't done it yet.

■ **Coaching requires the coach to believe in the client's capacity to achieve**
There are no conditions which are exceptions to this rule. The only variables are when and how. There are no 'ifs' in coaching.

■ **Coaching will be terminated if the coach is confident that the client does not have the will to change**
This should always be done with sensitivity and include referral to a more appropriate service if the coach believes the client needs help.

■ **Coaching will not continue if the coach suspects there are serious mental health issues affecting the client and which**

are not being addressed by other means

This is vital. Successful coaching requires a degree of toughness and insistence on achievement that could be damaging to a person made particularly vulnerable as a result of problems with mental health. However, it would be discriminatory to suggest that coaching is never appropriate for people with a recognised mental health problem. Many people who are accessing appropriate support for their particular illness could also benefit from good quality coaching.

Now you know what coaching is at its best you need to work on your coaching offer. In Chapter 2 you will have a chance to assess your own coaching skills, work out how to keep on developing as a coach and start thinking about how to keep your skills constantly updated.

2

Developing your coaching skills

This chapter will look at how you can develop your coaching skills both in formal training and in practice. Coaching is an increasingly competitive field. Your success in running a profitable, satisfying coaching practice will largely rest on three things:

1 Good results which generate word of mouth referrals.

2 Successful networking – making contacts which generate opportunities and referrals.

3 Keeping up to date with industry requirements.

However, qualifications and membership of professional organisations will soon start to be an important factor in gaining work. There are an increasing number of organisations employing people in roles which are all or partly about utilising coaching skills. Shortlisting applicants for exciting, well-paid jobs and deciding between competing bids for contracts is all about excluding people to achieve a manageable interview load. It is clear that employers and people seeking high quality bids for tenders (i.e. those looking for coaches to work on contract to deliver specific projects or objectives) or high-achieving staff for in-house coaching roles will soon, if not already, be forced to set the bar high to make their search manageable.

Before we look at the options in terms of training and accreditation, we will look at the personal side of putting yourself in the position of being a successful coach.

ARE YOU A SUCCESSFUL COACH?

I hope you said 'yes'. It does not matter how experienced or inexperienced you are at this stage of your career. You have to believe in your skills so that others believe in you too.

Have you ever been coached? If not by a personal coach then perhaps you worked with a coach in sport or a fitness coach to help you stick at an exercise regime? If you are lucky you will have worked with a coach who is obviously more concerned with the mind than with physical skills and technique. As a developing coach you can learn a lot from the way the best sports coaches focus on the mental approach of an athlete.

Most successful athletes talk about the importance of focus and of believing in themselves. The sprinter Linford Christie talked often about visualising the race, of seeing himself out in front of the field and crossing the finishing line first. It shouldn't be surprising that athletes focus on goals to get them through the gruelling years of training that underpin all successful athletic achievements. Even so, many of us do find it surprising when serious sportspeople attribute success not just to being physically well-prepared but also to their state of mind and their ability to visualise themselves winning.

The inner game

Timothy Gallwey coined the phrase 'the inner game', to capture the significance of the psychological aspects of achievement in sport. The crossover of relatively new ideas about maximising achievement in sports into the business environment is often attributed to his groundbreaking work. In Gallwey's book *The Inner Game of Tennis*, first published in 1974, he argued that a player who could win the 'inner game' would tap into a natural ability which would unleash latent skills and help turn them into a winner.

Gallwey was an early proponent of the idea that internal, psychological obstacles to achieving are often more damaging to our performance than external factors. So, for example, as a professional tennis player and coach Gallwey recognised that while a coach's expertise could be passed on to the player via advice and demonstration of the 'right' way to play a winning game this was not addressing what he called the 'opponent within one's own head'.

The game in our heads is all about overcoming the destructive and negative inner voice which most of us hear from time to time. You know the one. It tells you that you are useless at serving, that you are too tired to do your best and that your opponent is a Grand Slam champion so you don't stand a chance.

This is the voice which might be telling you that you are not sure you have what it takes to be an excellent coach or to run a successful coaching business. If you have this voice in your head you need to silence it sooner rather than later. If you have this voice in your life (for example a critical parent, an unsupportive partner or an unsettled teenage child who doesn't like to see you change) you need to tune it out because negative voices do make a difference if you let them. Remember limiting beliefs? We aren't born with them. No baby believes they'll never walk or talk. But many schoolchildren feel they won't ever do well in exams, get a good job, be a good person, and live out their dreams. They didn't just grow those ideas. Someone or some series of events planted the seed and the climate around them let the limiting beliefs flourish.

You are not a child. You have the power to change the microclimate around you. Make sure you do.

Chicken and egg

In the run up to the 2004 Olympics a senior British coach caused an outcry when he referred to the poor prospects of Britain in terms of medal wins. You might say that with friends like that who needs enemies, but the angry response from athletes to this unfortunate negative outburst highlighted the extent to which Gallwey's thinking (about the inner game) has influenced so many people.

Do you think that negative ideas can produce poor results? Or do poor results breed negative ideas? Instead of worrying about which came first – the chicken or the egg – take action. Negative ideas damage confidence and the idea that it is lack of confidence rather than lack of skill that often determines the difference between winning and losing is no longer widely disputed. The funny thing is that some of us find it a little bit harder to accept the implications of that idea for our own lives. Be your own coach and start combating any negative thoughts now.

Ditch the doomster

Are you 100 per cent confident about starting up your coaching business? Have you some fears or nagging doubts about being successful as a coach? Choose one example of a fear or a doubt your have about your future coaching career and write it here:

....

....

....

....

Now work out how to banish that fear by taking an appropriate action.

It might help you to work out how to do this if you better understand what is driving this concern.

■ What have people said about your taking up coaching and what did these comments (or lack of comments) mean to you?
■ How will you feel if you do not try this exciting adventure?
■ What evidence is there to suggest that you might fail?
■ What might you risk losing by taking the steps required to focus on coaching?

I will tackle my concerns/fears by ....

....

....

and I will do this by the following deadline: ....

DEVELOPING YOUR COACHING SKILLS

You may already have trained as a coach but this should not prevent you from exploring how to boost your skills. Evidence of continuing professional development (CPD) is what every professional person has to consider today. Employers will look for evidence of a willingness to keep on learning and people seeking to contract you as their coach will be looking for reassurance that your skills are up to date.

There are many ways of building coaching skills:

- You can be trained in coaching skills by an employer. This is increasingly common as employers seek to build coaching skills into the toolkit deployed by their managers.

- You can attend a course which offers a formal qualification such as a diploma.

- You can gain hands-on coaching experience – as a manager, as a volunteer or as a self-employed coach.

Employer training

My first coaching skills training took place when I was a manager in a large voluntary sector organisation. The organisation wanted to improve its pool of applicants for internal recruitments and was looking at ways of raising confidence levels and overcoming other barriers that prevented potentially great candidates from applying for jobs.

Several managers were recruited onto a special training scheme and given the title Career Coaches. It was our job to make time to listen to people who wanted to discuss career options, to help them explore career pathways in the organisation and, ultimately, to boost the number of internal applicants for posts.

Unfortunately, there was no qualification or certificate awarded at the end of the training. If your employer offers in-house training try to see if you can receive some sort of notice of achievement. Make sure, at the very least, that you keep a record of the coaching work you do in-house. Evidence of coaching hours is of growing importance. Coaches and counsellors are assessed a little like pilots. We aren't considered 'qualified' until we have a body of evidence showing that we have spent time coaching.

Keep your own coaching log which shows courses attended and which lists the time spent with every single client. Respect confidentiality by only identifying clients with initials or numbers so that you can show the log to anyone without betraying your clients or breaking any data protection rules.

Your coaching log is a valuable tool. Always keep it up to date. Look at the sample learning log provided here.

Coaching Log: Name				
Date of session	Client's initials or number	Paid or unpaid?	Length of session	Accumulated coaching hours
13.09.08	JP	Unpaid	40 mins	40 mins
13.09.08	SG	Paid	45 mins	1hr 25mins
14.09.08	MJ	Paid	45 mins	2hrs 10 mins
17.09.08	GK	Unpaid	15 mins	2hrs 25 mins

Coaching qualifications

Full-time, part-time, diploma, degree, certificate, distance learning, workplace learning, SVQs, NVQs – your head will be spinning by the time you have conducted a thorough search of all the training options out there.

The purpose of this section of the book is to provide a simple guide to types of courses, some useful contact details for gaining further information and some words of warning about certain types of coaching training.

Choosing between different training offers is challenging but there is one sure-fire way of narrowing down the options. Ask the kind of people you want to coach or organisations you want to coach for what qualifications they rate. After all, what's the point of attending the friendly, affordable course round the corner if the people you want to impress consider it to be of poor quality or to offer training they do not think relevant?

Distance learning

The advantages of distance learning are:

- Flexibility – you can fit study and practice into your current routine.

- Affordability – no travel costs or additional living expenses, and often lower course fees than those including face-to-face tutoring.

- Geography – you can study the best course without moving home.

The potential disadvantages of studying coaching by distance learning are:

- Lack of feedback on technique through practical skills work.

- Low standards – everyone passes.

- No recognised qualification or awards body not respected.

- Giving up because you have to work alone.

This book cannot recommend individual courses. I would be in terrible trouble if I started telling anyone what courses to avoid unless I had good quality evidence of their shortcomings. I am personally a great proponent of the distance learning option because it opens up initial and refresher training to people whose income and family circumstances just would not enable them to study full-time. I am the author of just such a course and I know that through studying this way my students learn the basic principles of coaching, the ethical aspects of coaching and the basics of how to start a coaching business. What I cannot offer them through this mode of learning is an assessment of their practical skills as a coach.

If distance learning appeals to you then you need to look for courses from reputable learning providers. You also need to consider very carefully how you will gain feedback on your practical coaching skills.

Three reputable providers currently offering distance learning options in coaching skills are:

1 **The Open University – www.open.ac.uk**. At the time of writing, it offers 'How to use coaching skills at work' a non-

Practical coaching skills and distance learning

My first coaching qualification, a Diploma in Life Coaching, came from a short weekend course which was backed up by a period of distance learning. Students were given feedback from an experienced coach/trainer on their coaching skills in exercises over the weekend. We then had to complete written assignments and submit them for assessment.

One huge advantage of this course over other distance learning opportunities was the development of coaching syndicate groups. We were assigned to a threesome during the course and required to work together when the weekend was over. We set up conference calls and took turns to coach each other on the telephone with one student acting as the listening observer. When each coaching session ended the coach and the observer stayed on the line after the coachee hung up. The observer fed back to the coach using carefully worked out feedback techniques.

This contributed greatly to the development of my practical coaching skills and I recommend seeking out courses that offer a similar opportunity. Or why not create your own coaching syndicates? Use web-based noticeboards to seek out volunteers

credit bearing course aimed at managers and other professional staff who coach people at work. The course is restricted to members of certain professional organisations and tied closely to workplace learning projects.

2   **The Chartered Institute of Personnel and Development (CIPD) – www.cipd.co.uk**. Several short courses and two distance learning courses were listed at the time of writing. For example, the CIPD Certificate in Coaching and Mentoring is billed as a 'highly practical programme that develops

understanding of both the theory and practice of coaching and mentoring'. It is described as being delivered through a blend of face to face, distance learning and online coaching methods, with emphasis on 'learning by doing'.

3   **ICS – www.icslearn.co.uk**. The course leading to the ICS Diploma in Life Coaching which sets out to teach proven techniques to build people's self-esteem and motivation and offers practical advice on setting up your own practice and attracting clients.

There are many other distance learning options, many of which combine some face-to-face coursework with study at home. More details are listed in the Useful Resources section at the end of this book. The cost of distance learning courses ranges from around the £500 mark to in excess of £5000. At the upper end the cost tends to reflect greater interaction with course tutors, more in-depth study opportunities with more detailed feedback and/or an association with a prestigious learning establishment.

As with all courses, your decision should be guided by as much firsthand knowledge as possible. Ask to speak to graduates and try to speak to at least three. This will give you a reasonably rounded picture of the strengths and weaknesses of the course you wish to study.

Full- and part-time courses

These can be the Rolls Royce options when it comes to initial training. But take the 'never mind the quality feel the width' approach at your peril. The institution offering the course might have a good general reputation or the qualification offered at the end of it might sound impressive but you must still do your research thoroughly. Ever heard of a 'cash cow'? Universities are under more pressure than ever to generate income and if they see a cash cow (i.e. a course lots of people will pay lots of money to attend) staff may be under pressure to milk it. So be as rigorous in your analysis of what the course offers as you would be if you were approaching an unknown learning provider. The following are key considerations.

- Ask graduates of the course for their feedback – preferably at least three.

- Ask the admissions team for feedback on the progress of graduates – are they working successfully as coaches?

- If you want to work in the corporate/executive coaching market, ask if the course has links with top companies for placements/workplace learning opportunities.

- If you want to work with another type of client, find out if the course will help you make contacts in the right field or will address the particular issues that coaching in this area might raise.

- Find out if the course offers any advantages after it is over – for example, an active alumni association to help with network-ing, links with professional bodies such as coach accreditation bodies, discounts on future courses which might help with your CPD.

- Ask about the tutors. The theory of coaching is not the same as the practice. Is the tutorial team staffed with experienced or active coaches? Will you be able to learn by professional example and not just from books and the performance of fellow students.

■ Find out about the course in more detail than the syllabus will give you. How much practical work (and therefore feedback on your performance) will you get? Some academic staff are very poor at organising group work and see it as a chance to disappear and catch up on marking or other tasks. You need honest, constructively critical feedback to develop as a coach. Your peers will be able to offer this but only if they are supported in so doing. This is the sort of group work a highly skilled facilitator will lead effectively – is there one of these involved in running the course?

■ Qualifications – what is the qualification you will gain at the end of the course and is it at the right level to help you meet your goals? Coaching qualifications range from certificates and diplomas right up to Master's degrees. Are you aiming for the level of qualification which meets your needs? For example, a Master's degree always sounds impressive but the workload will include activities and study which you might feel to be irrelevant to the business of coaching. This is because all Master's degrees need to meet certain academic standards which usually mean, for example, that there will be a research element in the assignments. Can you keep your motivation if you no longer see the relevance of the study to your goals? Only you can answer this question and make sure you do before embarking on a course.

■ Is the course flexible enough? Part-time attendance is a feature of most full-time courses in higher education so don't feel that you cannot ever study 'full-time' if you also have to work for your living. However, the workload will be deemed to be enough to keep you at least as busy as a full-time job so don't be fooled into thinking a two-days-a-week attendance requirement is a two-day-a-week workload. However, if you are a quick reader like me and enjoy writing assignments it is perfectly possible to work part-time and study 'full-time', and come out with a great result.

■ Are there any bursaries or other help with funding? University fees seem to be creeping up and up. Some institutions are better than others at seeking out financial help for mature students. Don't be shy about asking – some of the best students need extra help which is why higher education institutions work hard helping you access any funding that is available.

Not all courses are run by the university and college sector. There are a number of private providers in the coaching skills market. Most offer short courses, some offer longer periods of study. The same rules apply – do your homework and work out what they will contribute to helping you meet your goals.

What do experts say about coach training?

The Chartered Institute of Personnel and Development (CIPD), the professional body for those involved in the management and development of people, has produced a guide to organisations thinking of introducing coaching services. In advice about qualifications the report states that the 'reputation of the coaching industry has been weakened by training providers who claim to produce professional coaches from five-day training courses'. Although it goes on to state clearly that there is a place for short introductory courses, this statement should not be ignored. There is no doubt that HR managers looking to recruit coaching services will be looking increasingly for both a good quality initial qualification accredited by a respected institution and evidence of experience and learning gained from coaching practice.

As your career builds, your clients, particularly corporate clients, will look for evidence of CPD, possibly gained from refresher courses. Remember to budget for time out for learning and fees for courses when you develop your business plans.

For more information from the CIPD go to www.cipd.co.uk.

WHAT DO CLIENTS LOOK FOR IN A COACH?

For as long as coaching is not regulated in the UK there will be no requirement to acquire any specific level or type of training. It is obviously inadvisable to start out without any grounding in the art of coaching as this would be unfair and potentially harmful to your clients. However, this does not help you decide what level of initial training and continuing professional development would be right for you.

One easy way to help you work this out is to consider what clients look for in a coach. In essence this is simple. All clients, corporate and individual, will look for a track record of success. Therefore, one thing you should consider is how you build your own track record. This is where courses which offer practical, assessed coaching practice come into their own. A coach graduating from such a course will have an advantage over his or her peers.

Some clients will always want experience to be backed up by evidence of competence expressed through qualifications. While it is impossible to tell you what the best level or type of qualification is for someone wishing to run their own successful coaching business, what is offered here is some guidance on how potential clients will assess the merits of different coaches.

In its advice to HR managers the CIPD suggests that those looking to recruit or buy in coaching skills should look at several factors. These include:

- Does the coach have the **appropriate level of experience**? This means that if you are looking for someone to coach senior managers are you recruiting a coach who has worked with people in similar roles?

- Does the coach have **relevant industry/business experience**? For example, public sector organisations might have a very different culture than another type of business.

- Are good, relevant **references** available?

- What is the **background** of the coach? The CIPD has some evidence that coaches with a background in psychology are highly sought after because they will be able to better understand their clients and also be more likely not to miss or overlook serious psychological problems in their coachees.

- Does the coach have access to good quality, regular **supervision**? The practice of supervision, in which one professional regularly discusses challenges and other issues raised by their workload with another, usually more experienced professional, is common in the fields of counselling and therapy. The practice is patchy in the coaching industry. If you set up in business as a sole trader it is worth exploring how to set up a supervision arrangement. There is more information on this in Chapter 11.

- Does the coach offer a **number of tools, techniques and models**? This is about having a number of tools in your coaching toolkit. It highlights the importance of further training throughout your career as a coach and the advantage of seeking out initial training which introduces you to a variety of coaching models and tools.

■ Does the coach demonstrate a good understanding of **boundaries and approaches to referrals**? This is about showing you know when not to work with clients, for example, when poor mental health demands a different professional intervention.

■ Does the coach hold **relevant qualifications and training**? The CIPD is very specific on this topic and it is worth quoting from their advice which states:

The training of coaches should be fit for purpose. There is definitely a place for short introductory courses, but, as with any discipline, expertise will vary depending on the length of the course, level of qualification, depth of study, practical experience of delivery and extent of supervision and support received while studying. (Jessica Jarvis, *Coaching and Buying Coaching Services* – A CIPD Guide, p.48)

In addition the CIPD recommend HR managers to look at specific skills-based training. A good example of this would be a coaching project which was aimed at helping an individual develop their presentation skills. Wouldn't you want to know whether the coach had some knowledge or experience in a similar field and wouldn't you look for evidence of presentation skills training somewhere in their CV?

■ The CIPD also suggests that **membership of professional bodies** is relevant. At the same time it freely admits that this isn't a guarantee of competence. However, the CIPD sensibly points out that among the plethora of organisations putting themselves forward to be *the* professional body for coaches, most have codes of conducts to which members are required to subscribe. This is reassuring to clients. This suggests that you should consider checking with professional bodies about their recommendations or standards relating to qualifications and experience. There is more information on this on pages 35–44.

▪ Does the coach hold adequate **professional indemnity insurance**? Insurance is not only valuable to you, ensuring that in an increasingly litigious climate you are not bankrupted by a claim against you, it is also a sign of your seriousness and professionalism.

▪ What is your assessment of the coach's **other qualities and personal characteristics**? The CIPD draws attention to the European Mentoring and Coaching Council's (EMCC) map of knowledge, skills and behaviours that are required or desirable in a coach. These include attributes such as self-awareness, flexibility of approach and listening skills. There is more information on the EMCC and other relevant organisations in Chapter 3.

So how does this help you to understand what qualifications you need and what course to choose? The point of reproducing this list is to show you that qualifications are just one aspect of a long list of factors under consideration by your potential clients. Once you start making connections between these factors you will quickly come to some useful conclusions about what qualifications to aim for. Perhaps the single most important question to ask yourself is this: Is the qualification and the means by which I will gain this qualification fit for my particular purposes?

The following checklist is designed to help you reach a decision about the qualification that is right for you. If you cannot answer the questions by studying the prospectus these are questions you can ask of the course admissions staff.

Question	Yes or No
Does the course lead to a qualification recognised by an accreditation body I would like to join?	
Does the course involve practical skills work and theoretical work in a range of settings and with a range of different types of client?	
Does the course cover psychological theory to a level which will enable me to work safely with clients because I will be able to spot potentially serious issues?	
Does the course offer supervision of trainee coaches?	
Does the course offer any means of sustaining a supervisory relationship for a period after graduation?	
Does the course teach a number of tools, techniques and models for coaching?	
Does the course fit with my goals in terms of cost and duration?	
Does the qualification open routes into further study?	

WORKING AS A VOLUNTEER

This is a tried and tested route for boosting skills and levels of experience. Volunteering is not just an option for beginners. Experienced coaches seeking to expand into new markets can build up experience and references by volunteering their coaching skills in the new area before trying to obtain paid work. However, don't assume that beggars can't be choosers and that organisations seeking volunteer coaches will take just anybody. Many voluntary sector organisations are highly experienced in recruiting and managing volunteers. They have a strong ethical dimension to their work and would not dream of letting an inexperienced coach loose on possibly vulnerable clients. Indeed you may find that the recruitment criteria for volunteers and the demands on you in terms of participating in training, reporting and supervision are higher than those applied in the private and paid sector.

Having said that, this does make volunteering highly attractive to those coaches seeking to boost their skills level and gain recognition for the work that they do. Private clients may provide you with glowing testimonials but at the end of the day they are like those junk mail competition winners. Nobody knows who they are and the cynical among us might well wonder if you invented them purely for the purposes of boosting your CV. Established voluntary sector organisations have their reputation firmly in mind when they provide references. As an employer myself I rate very highly a positive reference from such an organisation because I judge them to be honest and reliable.

Never underestimate the buzz you will get from working towards the social good. One of the exciting aspects of voluntary coaching is that you get to work with clients who could never afford your fees. Coaching and mentoring skills are currently in high demand in the following areas:

- Projects designed to support people in moving from welfare benefits and back into work.

- Projects targeting young people who are not in employment, education or training.

- Projects designed to reduce youth offending.

Many of the organisations working in these areas use a mix of paid staff and volunteers.

How do I find coaching work as a volunteer?

Some organisations will advertise volunteer vacancies in national newspapers and magazines. The *Guardian* publishes advertisements for volunteer positions in its G2 section on Wednesdays and the *Big Issue* also publishes adverts for recruiting volunteers. In Scotland, such vacancies are often listed in the *Herald* on Tuesdays and the *Scotsman* on Fridays. Volunteer vacancies are also advertised on job recruitment websites. These include www.goodmoves.org.uk and www.s1jobs.com (in Scotland).

Some organisations will rely on word of mouth or on recruitment systems run by their local volunteer centre. It is always worth writing to or phoning organisations which offer coaching or mentoring or which work with a client group on an issue of interest to you and offering your services. If you have a lot of time to spare then try typing 'volunteer vacancies' into the Google search engine. I did this at the time of writing and it generated more than 54,000 hits for the UK alone. The range of coaching-type volunteer placements extended from mentoring ex-offenders to coaching people over a period of eight months to help them in the process of finding employment.

Key websites for researching volunteering opportunities using a more targeted approach are:

www.volunteering,org.uk – for opportunities in England
www.volunteerscotland.org.uk – for opportunities in Scotland
www.volunteernow.org.uk – for opportunities in Northern
    Ireland
www.volunteering-wales.net – for opportunities in Wales.

Remember, although most voluntary sector organisations are very short of money they do try to meet very high standards in their employment practices. This means that most will cover expenses incurred while volunteering and many will offer training to help you meet the requirements of the volunteer role.

Lots of coaches ask me how they will get essential practical experience to help them develop as a coach. I always recommend volunteering. A combination of a course leading to a qualification and the training and experience on offer from a well-run voluntary sector organisation will certainly help you meet the criteria outlined by the CIPD and put you well on the road to being offered those all-important paid roles and contracts.

IS MEMBERSHIP OF A PROFESSIONAL BODY ESSENTIAL?

Coaching differs from other forms of development because the coach is working without the benefit of colleagues immediately available for support, and the nature of the relationship is such that coaches carry significant responsibility, which they have to deal with alone. Accreditation provides assurance to clients that their coach is up to the task, and provides support and continuing development for the coaches themselves. (Ashridge Business School, March 2008, www.ashridge.org.uk/Website/Con tent.nsf/wCOA/Accreditation?opendocument)

This explains in a nutshell why potential clients are anxious to find a way of ensuring that the coaches they recruit will work to a good standard. Whether you are coaching an individual in a corporate context or a private client it can be very hard for the client to assess the quality of what's on offer. It can also be very hard for the coach to gain sufficient critical distance from the task in hand, or support from others, to ensure their work is and continues to be of a high standard.

Ashridge Business School is one of very many UK-based organisations currently offering to underwrite the quality of coaches associated with them. Although the school has an excellent reputation, it is only one of many that offer an accreditation scheme to coaches and those buying coaching services. According to the Coaching and Mentoring Network (www.coachingnetwork.org.uk) there are at least 23 UK-based universities and colleges offering accredited coaching courses.

In its 2004 report on buying in coaching services the CIPD named four coach membership organisations, which both required members to adhere to an ethical code and provided a complaints procedure. There are several more organisations promoting a similar service and no obvious frontrunner in terms of standards and reputation for the time being.

Regulation of coaching in the UK

The CIPD cites membership of a professional body, possession of relevant qualifications and evidence of continuing professional development as three key criteria in the selection process. In light of this advice it is clearly advantageous for coaches to join a professional body. However, there is no legal obligation to do so and this lack of regulation makes choosing a membership organisation quite challenging. The lack of a recognised governing body for coaching and the sheer number of organisations competing to recruit coaches as their members poses a number of difficulties.

This lack of a recognised authority to regulate the activities of coaches has a parallel in the field of counselling. In February 2005, the Department of Health funded the British Association for Counselling and Psychotherapy and the United Kingdom Council for Psychotherapy (UKCP) to carry out research into the provision of counselling and psychotherapy training in the UK and the standards of that training and the codes of ethics and practice, and conduct processes of all registering/accrediting counselling and psychotherapy organisations. This was no small task as there are quite a few accrediting and registering bodies in the field just as there are in coaching.

In 2007 the UK government signalled its firm intention to regulate counselling and psychotherapy services. Some say it is long overdue. In the UK it has long been the case that anyone, no matter how inexperienced and under-trained, could call themselves a counsellor and set up in business. Sound familiar? This is exactly the current case with coaching.

Does this matter? I believe it does. Coaching relationships can be intense and there is some scope for coaches to exploit or harm clients. I would argue that the risks of abuse are generally much lower than with therapeutic work if only because clients are generally not in an especially vulnerable state. However, people who are lacking in confidence, people who are or have been depressed and people who feel disempowered do invest in coaching. A skilful, ethical coach will avoid creating feelings of dependency in their clients and work to boost confidence. A manipulative, unethical coach may choose to do the opposite. An unskilled, inexperienced coach may cause harm unintentionally but it is the potential to cause harm not the story behind it that suggests the need for standards to be set in coaching.

I do not believe that regulation always raises standards. It may set the bar higher in terms of entry to a profession but when regulations are poorly designed or policed they serve no one's interests. Without a regulatory framework to fall back on you must make your own choices.

Three ways of signalling quality to your clients

If you want to provide assurance of the quality of your work to potential clients there are three key steps it is advisable to take. These are:

1   Qualify as a coach, or take further training, under the auspices of, an organisation with a good reputation for high standards of learning, which offers qualifications properly accredited by a mainstream learning provider and which offers a coach accreditation scheme and/or ongoing supervision.

2   Join a professional body that requires of its members the adoption of an ethical code and which operates a complaints and disciplinary procedure designed to improve standards and/or weed out poor quality coaches.

3   Build up a substantial portfolio of testimonials from satisfied clients and work with clients whose recommendations will be taken seriously by others in their field.

The trouble is that this still leaves you with the challenge of choosing which organisation to train with, to join and to rely on for accrediting your work as a coach. It might help to stand in a prospective client's shoes. Ask yourself this: How would I choose a coach?

Or, turn the question around. If you were not acting on a personal recommendation from someone whose judgment you trust ask: what would make a potential coach stand out as being a coach I would trust?

I would look for some sort of evidence of their professional skills. I would hope to be able to rely on some sort of independent corroboration of their claims in this area. If you feel the same way it suggests a way forward which will help build your coaching business.

There is one further question you should ask. If you have a major client already, or you are targeting a specific client or client area, then you should ask: which organisation would my client(s) expect me to be a member of?

Advantages of membership of professional bodies

To help you make this decision it is worth considering a number of important benefits membership of the right organisation might bring to you. So far we have only looked at the role some form of accreditation or membership might play in reassuring clients of your suitability as a coach for them. It is also well worth considering further potential advantages membership organisations might bring to you. These could include:

1   Networking opportunities with other coaches.

2   Confidence from belonging to a respected organisation.

3   Publicity for your coaching services.

4   Access to good quality courses and latest research for CPD.

5   Special deals on indemnity and/or public liability insurances.

6   Support in handling client complaints.

7   Advice and early warning on legal and policy matters relating to running a coaching business.

8   A chance to influence policy via your membership organisation.

9   Guidance on running a small business.

Only you can judge which, if any, of these potential benefits is important to you. Once you have a good idea of what membership of a recognised coaching accreditation/membership body can do for you make sure you rank your requirements in order of priority.

Researching membership bodies

Now research the field to find out which organisation most closely meets your requirements.

I am not going to direct you to a specific membership organisation. To do so when there are several apparently reputable organisations offering similar levels of service to members and to coaching clients would be unfair. The best I can do is to point you in the direction of some organisations that clearly define an ethical code by which members must abide and offer a complaints and disciplinary procedure for the handling of formal complaints about members.

International Coach Federation – www.coachfederation.org

Guarantees that member coaches:

■ have received professional training from a programme specifically designed to teach coaching skills in alignment with the ICF Competencies and Code of Ethics

■ have demonstrated a proficient understanding and use of the coaching competencies as outlined by the ICF

■ are accountable to the ethics and standards set forth by the ICF.

Association for Professional Executive Coaching and Supervision – www.apecs.org

Guarantees that member coaches will:

■ be properly qualified to carry out the work (see APECS Accreditation Criteria Guidelines)

■ ensure that the requirements of the coaching/supervision contract are within their professional ability to deliver or make clear to the client and the sponsor where the shortfall may be

■ continue to learn and grow in their professional knowledge and expertise

■ invest in personal development work to enhance their self-awareness and emotional balance

■ work with an approved supervisor (see APECS Accreditation Criteria Guidelines) to ensure client safety, review their client case work and monitor their own well-being and effectiveness.

Association for Coaching – www.associationfor coaching.com

Associate membership is restricted to coaches with at least 75 hours' coaching experience or evidence of 35 hours' training plus 40 hours' practice. Affiliate membership has less stringent requirements and full membership requires evidence of a minimum of 250 hours' coaching practice or a combination of training and coaching practice adding up to 250 hours. References are required to secure associate and full membership.

The Association has a clear set of ethical guidelines for members. These include a requirement on coach members to engage in at least 30 hours of CPD every year.

The Association's members must let clients know about the Association's complaints procedures if they become aware that a client is unhappy with the service the coach has provided. The Association commits to investigating complaints which are deemed to refer to any breach of the Association's Code of Ethics.

European Mentoring and Coaching Council – www.emccouncil.org

The EMCC offers a number of modes of membership which require adoption of the Council's Code of Ethics. The Code makes a number of requirements of the Council's members including:

- operating at all times within their level of competence

- maintaining a relationship with a suitably qualified supervisor who will regularly assess their competence

- maintaining appropriate and agreed levels of confidentiality in coaching relationships

- representing their qualifications, experience and competence honestly to clients and in published work.

The Council offers a complaints and disputes resolution service to its members. In cases where complaints indicate a breach of its ethical code the Council will step in where direct contact between coach and client has failed to resolve complaints.

Coaching Psychology Forum – www.sgcp.org.uk

This organisation, known also as the Special Group in Coaching Psychology, grew out of the growth in numbers of psychologists who are members of the British Psychological Society with an interest in coaching. All qualified graduate members of the British Psychological Society are bound by ethical guidelines.

The Forum reports that it is also open to non-psychologist coaches who are interested in the appropriate application of psychological theory and methods to coaching practice. The website states that:

Coaches who are not psychologists are welcome to join the SGCP provided they become affiliate members of the BPS. An affiliate member of the BPS does not need to have any formal psychological training, but must demonstrate a genuine interest in the theory and practice of psychology.

3

My Dream Business

This chapter is all about helping you create a vision of a business that fits with the life you want to live. It helps you explore what you want to get from running your coaching business and what it will take to get there.

The rest of the book will provide some practical advice on ways of working, targeting specific client groups and how to plan your business in detail. Before you go there it will help if you take time out to make sure you know what you want and have imagined a number of ways of getting there.

Successful businesspeople are nearly always passionate about what they do. They are often prepared to work long hours and take significant financial risks to build up their businesses. Do you feel that way about starting up a coaching business?

If not, then all is not lost. You do need energy and passion to make a success of coaching but you do not need to take huge financial risks or work very long hours to run a business which meets your needs.

A BUSINESS THAT FITS YOUR LIFE GOALS

In coaching it is sometimes necessary to be clear about which goals are END goals and which are PROCESS goals.

END goals are your ultimate destination. These are the big achievements which can take a long time to work towards. PROCESS goals are steps on this journey. Sometimes people decide that running a successful business is their END goal. Everything else ranks below this major life goal.

For some of us starting up a coaching business is more of a PROCESS goal. A step we are taking towards achieving a more flexible workload so that we can free up time or increase our income to enable us to achieve goals in other areas of our life. Do you see your coaching business as being:

■ A step on the way to achieving change in several areas of your life?

■ Your main goal in life, you want to be a successful entrepreneur?

Your chances of starting up a coaching business that meets your needs will be increased immeasurably if you make sure you know exactly what you want out of life in general and your business in particular.

Don't panic – we are all allowed to change our life goals from time to time. It just increases your chances of dreaming up a business you truly love if you know what exactly you want to get from that business right now and in the foreseeable future. Try answering these questions:

■ What do you want to achieve in life?
■ How will running a coaching business help you get there?

When you know these two things you can start planning for a business that is right for the life you want to live.

Do you have some clear goals for what you want to achieve in life? If not, go back to Chapter 1 and work through some of the exercises there.

PLANNING: FIRST STEPS

The following questions will help you start planning your business:

- What do I want to get from running my own coaching practice?
- How much time do I want to spend on running this business?
- How much money do I want to make from running this business?

There are some examples of what running a coaching practice can offer in the box below. Take a moment to consider which of these are most important to you. Are there more you want to add?

Starting and running a coaching business will bring me:

- ☐ Better work–life balance
- ☐ Flexible hours
- ☐ Autonomy
- ☐ Challenging/satisfying work
- ☐ Opportunity to grow my income
- ☐ New skills and experience
- ☐ More self-respect
- ☐ Respect of others
- ☐ Opportunity to become an employer
- ☐ Low cost business start-up
- ☐ Chance to work alone
- ☐ ....
- ☐ ....

Working to live/living to work?

Coaches often work with people who are seeking a better work–life balance. Before you start planning the business itself it is vital you set yourself clear goals relating to your work–life balance.

What does achieving a better work–life balance mean to you? The Work Foundation says that:

> *Work-life balance is about people having a measure of control over when, where and how they work. It is achieved when an individual's right to a fulfilled life inside and outside paid work is accepted and respected as the norm, to the mutual benefit of the individual, business and society.* (www.employersforwork-life-balance.org.uk/work/definition.htm, accessed 22 June 2007)

All of us benefit from having some control over when, where and how we work but what makes for a 'fulfilled life inside and outside paid work' varies enormously from one person to another.

For some people a better work–life balance might mean more work. For others it might mean more time out of work to enjoy other aspects of life. Some of us are happiest working hard in an intellectually challenging job but only want to work half the week. Others don't mind how many hours they spend in paid work as long as that work doesn't demand so much of them that they leave feeling drained and fit for nothing else.

All businesses require a lot of input in the early days. The point is to know what you are aiming to achieve with your business. What do you want your business to provide for you in the short, medium and long term?

If you are not already clear about your aims in the area of work–life balance try working through the life balance chart below and think about:

- What it tells you about how you would like to spend your time.
- What it tells you about what kind of work you find fulfilling.

Flexible hours

Running your own coaching business does not mean you can always pick and choose the hours you work. Issues which will affect your hours of work (other than your personal preferences) include:

- Your chosen target client. For example, executive coaching can be during normal business hours but some busy people prefer early morning or evening appointments. If you really hate working evenings or weekends research your target market carefully to find out what that client group expects and demands.

- Working in a partnership or employing others. As soon as you take this step you will find it necessary to compromise on working hours. Expect conflict if you try to meet only your own needs.

- Income targets. There is always a relationship between your chosen client target group, the rates they are willing to pay for coaching and your desired income. High income targets and low paying clients equal more time at work than you might desire. Think carefully about how to balance these three crucial elements when you plan your business.

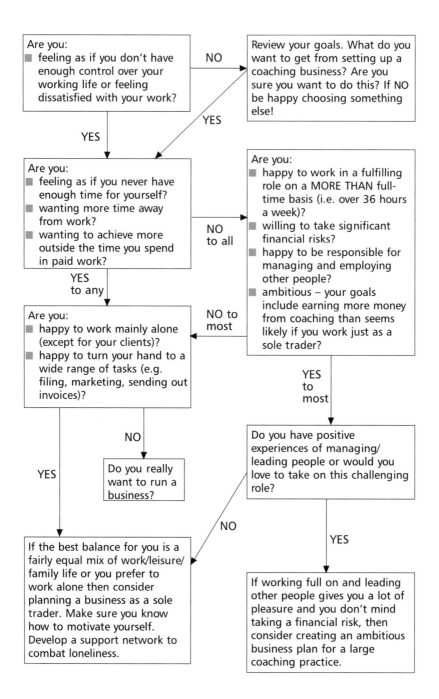

Life balance chart

■ Peaks and troughs. Some client groups are more likely to present you with peaks and troughs of business. For example, if you choose to focus on coaching in health and fitness you will benefit from all those New Year's resolutions. But will you want to work really hard for some months of the year and then take time out when it's quieter? It's up to you to sort this out at the planning stage.

Autonomy and working alone

To be one's own master is to be the slave of self. (Natalie Clifford Barney, www.answers.com/topic/autonomy?cat=health; accessed 22 June 2007)

That's all that needs to be said really. When you seek autonomy at work then beware of becoming the worst boss you ever had. Avoid this by:

■ planning for time off and taking it
■ never letting fear of failure become your only motivator.

You must be honest with yourself about your capacity to work alone. If you choose to set up a small business as a sole trader then you will not have colleagues around you for support and fun. Think about:

■ How much you might miss 'water cooler gossip' and office social life.

■ How you will get positive feedback for work well done.

■ How you will let off steam on a bad day.

■ Who you will discuss challenges at work with given that client sessions are confidential.

■ How you will pick yourself up off the floor when one too many potential clients turns down the idea of working with you.

Some of these matters can be addressed by finding another coach who will respect confidentiality and who might also be a useful mentor. Some of the potentially negative impacts of working alone can be tackled by ensuring that you enjoy a good level of social contact outside work.

Ultimately you might not be cut out for working alone. If this seems possible then consider planning for a larger business in which you either employ or work in partnership with other coaches.

CHALLENGING/SATISFYING WORK

Coaching is always challenging and so is running your own business. Unfortunately, not all challenges are ones we relish. For example, coaching an under-confident 21-year-old into her first steps on the career ladder might give you a buzz. But will you feel the same way about organising your business finances or dealing with your tax return?

> **Find out more about the work of running a business by:**
>
> ■ *meeting and listening to as many small business owners as you can*
> ■ *shadowing the CEO of a larger consultancy organisation that offers coaching as one of its services*
> ■ *reading the biographies of entrepreneurs who built their own small or large businesses*
> ■ *meeting and listening to other coaches who are already running their own coaching businesses.*

Be honest with yourself about the work involved in running a business. What will you enjoy, what will give you a feeling of satisfaction and how can you plan to reduce the burden of the tasks you find less than joyful and fulfilling?

If you do not know much about running a business at this stage think about ways in which you can find out more about what it is really like.

RESPECT

There is no doubt about it, starting up a successful morally and ethically sound business is an achievement that commands respect in our culture. This is probably because people understand that all business start-ups involve an element of risk. Your self-respect will soar if you pull off the dream of running your own successful business.

However, if you choose to work alone or to achieve modest income goals the obvious signs of that respect from others might be thin on the ground. Firstly your work might be largely invisible to everyone but you and your clients. Secondly, as the gap between rich and poor has accelerated in recent years, the ability to acquire vast amounts of money and live a lavish lifestyle often seems to be what people respect the most.

We all desire other people's respect but some of us need this respect to be clearly signalled in order to feel good about ourselves. In a senior role in a hierarchical organisation this 'respect' is encoded in our job title, our higher than average salaries, the fact we are asked to take on special roles or to give others the benefit of our wisdom or time. This can be very rewarding (and sometimes quite stressful as well, particularly if we feel unworthy of the attention).

Think about your true desire and your inner needs. Running a small business as a sole trader can be a little bit like parenting. Everyone knows it is an important job but the financial rewards are often quite low and the work appears to be largely invisible to most other people.

How will you cope with the changes that running your business might bring in terms of how you are seen by others? How will it affect your confidence and self-respect?

OPPORTUNITY TO GROW MY INCOME

Yes, starting a coaching business often enables people to significantly increase their income. This will almost certainly be true for you if you decide to start a part-time business without leaving your current employment. However, if you decide to take the plunge and commit to building a full-time coaching business you must make sure you have a solid grasp of the financial facts and figures.

Core issues which are often overlooked by people moving into self-employment are:

- the costs of covering time off for holidays and illness

- the costs of maintaining pension provision

- the costs of insurance, such as professional indemnity insurance

- the costs of your unpaid time which must be spent on administration. This includes keeping your accounts, dealing with tax issues, marketing your business. A good rule of thumb is to allow 20 per cent of your time for these matters.

This is one whole day in a five-day working week

■ the costs of running an office, such as heating, computer consumables, broadband and telephone charges.

Make sure you have a very clear understanding of the relationships between:

■ the type of clients you want to coach and their capacity to pay your fees

■ the hours you can work, the hours you want to work and the income you want to make

■ the costs you will incur and the gross income you believe it is possible to generate.

OPPORTUNITY TO BECOME AN EMPLOYER

Some coaches are content to run their coaching business alone. Others want to expand and assume the best way to grow the business is to employ other coaches. The obvious point here is that businesses can only remain profitable if they pay their staff less than those people generate in income.

Make sure you know the real cost and the legal

Innovative ways to grow

When Anita Roddick started the Body Shop the chain grew in the early days through franchising. This meant the costs of setting up new shops was born by the franchisee and not the parent company. Another model is to grow as a co-operative. Co-operatives are coming back into fashion. The Phone Co-op, a highly successful telecomms provider with strong ethical and environmental principles, was set up in 1998 and now has a turnover of £5 million.

Employees and customers can become members of the co-op and have some say over how the business is run. Partnerships are also a tried and tested route to business growth.

responsibilities which apply when employing people before assuming this is going to be easy. You might be happy to work 52 weeks of the year but you cannot legally make your staff do the same. You might even risk working without adequate insurance or good health and safety measures in place. You cannot get away with 'winging it' once you become an employer.

You also need to be sure that managing people is what you want to do with your time. Be clear about how much of your time you want to spend on coaching clients and how much on enabling others to do their best work.

Finally, be creative and imagine a number of ways of growing your business. There are plenty of successful businesses which have taken innovative routes to growth. Find out about them and start dreaming.

CREATING A VISION FOR YOUR COACHING BUSINESS

Skip this part if you already know exactly what type of coaching business you want to build. You are ready to move on to creating your detailed business plan.

Some of you will need to go away now and create the perfect environment for dreaming up your ideal business. Good ways of unleashing your creativity include:

- taking an invigorating shower or relaxing bath
- going for a long walk somewhere quiet and on your own
- lying in the sun
- going for a long drive alone
- gardening
- listening to music

■ bouncing ideas off a non-judgmental acquaintance that you can trust to be positive rather than throwing up barriers. Now is the time to dream – you can deal with the likely challenges later.

Some of you might like to have some source material to help guide your thinking. Try reading the following case studies. Is there an example here that comes close to how you see yourself and your business?

However you get to it, creating a clear vision of your coaching business and keeping it in mind throughout the planning process will help you construct a business plan that makes sense for you.

STELLAR ACHIEVEMENTS

Stellar Achievements is the brainchild of former city banker Stella Morris. In just three years Stella has built a coaching business with a £2 million turnover and now employs a team of 30 executive coaches specialising in revitalising the careers of executives at risk of total burnout. She made a small profit last year and is planning further growth over the next three years.

'I put everything I had into the business,' says Stella. 'I risked my house to get the start-up capital I needed and had sleepless nights knowing I owed the bank several hundred thousand pounds.'

Stella jokes that her two young children think their mummy never sleeps. 'I've always been there for them when they needed me even if it's meant working all night on a client presentation or writing up staff appraisals at dawn.'

Will she cash in by selling up now the business is making profits at last? Stella says not. 'I just love the buzz of working with my team. I wouldn't know what to do with myself if I took time out.'

Go4Goals

Go4Goals aims to help young people struggling with life and career choices. Gordon Preston trained as a coach while still working as a secondary school teacher in South Lanarkshire because he wanted to be able to offer more help to today's troubled teens.

'I saw so many children failing to make the most of their time at school and I often felt they just needed someone to help them find some motivation. The trouble is teachers don't have the time to help every student on a one-to-one basis.'

Gordon started his business on a part-time basis three years ago. At first he relished the extra cash but at just £25 a session, which is all he felt his client group could afford, he knew that coaching full-time wasn't going to pay the bills.

'I was anxious about giving up a good salary. There's no holiday or sickness pay if you are self-employed and I had my own family's needs to consider. That's when I thought about starting up a social business,' explains Gordon. 'I had all the evidence from my previous clients. I knew that coaching could help students improve their results at school.'

Gordon approached several organisations asking for grant funding to subsidise his work with young people. He now runs his not-for-profit business full-time on a grant funded salary but is thinking of seeking a job-share partner so he can free up some extra time for his family.

GRACE O'MALLEY COACHING

Mother of three Grace O'Malley launched her coaching business last year.

'I like to work with parents,' she says. 'I feel I understand the challenges they face and I get a huge buzz out of helping people turn their lives around.'

Grace started her business when her oldest child turned five. Before that she worked full-time as an NHS manager.

'I could see that school holidays were going to be difficult to cover. It's not like full-time nursery care and we didn't want our kids to have to cope with lots of different childcare arrangements.'

Luckily for Grace and her partner Joe they were both able to switch to part-time hours in their main jobs.

'It means we have the whole week covered for childcare which is great but we had to do something to cope with quite a dramatic fall in income.'

Grace chose coaching because she could work with clients in the evenings and because she could reduce her workload during school holidays.

'It's not as easy as you think. I do have to market myself and sort out the admin side of running a small business. I'd say this takes about a half a day a week, sometimes more. But I love coaching although I think I'd find it too draining if I tried to do it every day.'

Do any of these examples come close to the vision you are creating of your perfect coaching business?

Keep hold of your vision while we move into a discussion of one of the most important aspects of planning your business. This is the challenging matter of business growth.

GROWING YOUR BUSINESS

When people ask the infamous 'dragons' on BBC's *Dragon's Den* for investment in their business one of the common questions asked in return is 'Is this business scaleable?' This question is about the potential for any business to grow. Investors obviously seek growth in a business because they are looking for a good return on their investment. They want the business scaled up because large profits are unlikely to come from small businesses.

But when you are running your own business and do not have to satisfy any external investors you should always question what growth will get for you. Do you want a business that grows or are you happy to keep things on a small scale? This question is not as simple as it seems. One really important point you must be clear about is what 'growth' means to you.

What do you mean by growth?

For example, a coaching business that generates 100 coaching sessions at £50 per session each year would generate a reasonable part-time income. If you wanted this part-time income to keep pace with inflation so that you did not become progressively poorer year on year you would have two main choices:

1   Increase the session price to match the rate of inflation so that the money you earn each year has the same buying power.

2   Increase the number of client sessions you coach each year.

In the first case your business is not growing, neither is your spending power. In the second case your business is growing and your spending power might also grow depending on how many extra coaching sessions you run.

Of course you might choose a mixture of both strategies. For example, this might be necessary if you felt your client market would baulk at paying increased charges.

But what if you want to achieve more than just keep pace with inflation? What if you want to grow the business:

- so that you can sell it and generate a lump sum to invest in other ventures or in your pension?

- so that you can share responsibility for running it with others?

- so that it generates a higher income for you and your family?

- so that it can continue running and generating an income for you after you retire?

Ideally you should be clear about your immediate, mid- and long-term goals before you even start your business. Planning for growth is possible at any stage of the life cycle of your business. However, you'll be far more likely to get to where you want to be when you want to be there if you have clear business growth goals right from the start of your business venture.

This takes us back to first principles; What do you want to get from setting up and running your own coaching business? If you haven't answered this question by now then go back to the beginning of this chapter and take some time to think about your dream business now.

Your personal goals and your goals for your business are the key to working out what you mean by and what you plan to do about growing your business.

Going for growth

If you want more than a stable, inflation-proof, part-time income you will need to grow your business. This will demand that you:

- have a clear set of goals for growth
- a strategy for how you will grow the business.

If your vision for the business is that it will grow to involve others in delivering the work of the business you will also have to:

- develop the skills you need to delegate tasks and responsibilities to others

- give up controlling your business and take up managing the business

- trust others to deliver agreed outcomes.

There are other implications too. Running a business is very time consuming. Now, imagine running the business as it is while at the same time scaling it up. There will be extra work. This will include:

- Developing the strategy for growth.

- Developing the skills you need to deliver on this strategy.

- Securing any additional investment needed, then managing investors and their expectations.

- Recruiting then managing and supporting partners or staff.

- Recruiting additional clients.

- Dealing with new amounts of paperwork and new matters such as registering for VAT, running or contracting out a payroll service for staff, providing or managing a Human Resources function to support staff, overseeing the health and safety of others, leasing office space, ensuring cash flow is adequate to cover regular financial commitments such as wages, utility bills, etc.

Every small business owner has to work hard to cover all the bases in the early days. Small business owners with plans for significant business growth will find that they must work even harder. There will be stages when you are juggling so many roles and responsibilities that the sheer effort of getting through one day will be more of a challenge than any day's work you've ever done. This is the time when you will have to be able to keep your eyes on whatever prize you're after. You have to be able to answer the question: what is it all for?

WHAT IS IT ALL FOR?

I think it probably is the case that no one nearing the end of their life ever says that they wish they had spent more time at the office. But that doesn't mean that many of us won't wind up wishing we had taken a few more risks, or worked a bit harder to get to a place we once dreamed about.

Once you start your business you will need to decide how much time and energy you will devote to maintaining it and to growing it. We will return to this subject in Chapter 9 which will explore the typical life cycle of a growing business and give you ideas and advice for handling each stage. It is written in the firm belief that if you want to grow your coaching business you then you will be able to do it.

Who do you want to coach?

4

Who do you want to coach? Be honest, are you really all that interested in the ups and downs of the middle management life? Do ladies who have little more to do than lunch while desperately seeking some meaning and purpose in life make your hackles raise? Are you able to remain non-judgmental in the presence of a troubled teen that has just walked out of their umpteenth job because he or she didn't like getting up so early?

Stereotypes these may be, but your work as a coach will be more successful if you are clear about what sort of people you want to coach and where you will find them. Some of the most successful businesses in the world developed out of their founder's hobby or passion. There are several reasons for this:

- Enthusiasm generates energy and the will to succeed.

- Knowledge helps build confidence which is essential when pitching to investors/clients.

- Access to networks and relevant expertise helps build robust businesses.

If you know a lot about a specific subject area or client group you will:

- know where to find them
- know how best to reach them
- find it easier to plug into relevant networks
- be able to build trust quickly with clients
- have existing contacts you can use to build your business
- possibly have experience or qualifications seen as relevant to the field.

You might still choose to target an area of special interest even if you have none of these advantages. The one thing to avoid is targeting a specialist coaching market in which the clients are people you already know you will not enjoy working with. The one common factor to all successful coaching interactions is the faith a coach must be able to place in his or her clients. If you do not believe that a client has the will and the ability to set and reach their goals then you should not be working with them. It is not easy to sustain this positive belief in clients if we have strong negative feelings about 'people like them'. You know that coaches should not be judgmental but we are all just human. Be honest about your prejudices, be prepared to tackle them, never let them affect your coaching and make that easier by ensuring you do not focus on a special interest area that is not right for you.

WHAT ARE THESE SPECIAL INTEREST AREAS?

Every year I receive business plans to assess from students studying a distance learning course in coaching. Every student is required to identify their target market. Their choices fall largely into three categories:

1   Markets defined by age, gender, life stage or geography. E.g.:
    –   women looking to return to work after caring for children

– people in the Reading area
– people aged 50+ planning for retirement.

2   Markets defined by relationships to work. E.g.:
– people seeking a career change
– students seeking their first job.

3   Markets defined by special interest. E.g.:
– people on long-term sick leave
– people wanting to lose weight
– people wanting to improve their sports performance
– young people not in employment, education or training
– people wanting to give up smoking.

Clearly there is overlap between these categories. The 55-year-old coming up for retirement may well have as one of his or her goals 'to run a marathon in under four hours' or 'to give up smoking'. The purpose of identifying the category of 'special interest' is to help you think through how and why focusing on coaching in an area of special interest might help you to run a successful coaching business.

To help you think through an area of special interest which it might be worth exploring before planning your business this chapter will focus on three topical areas – health, sports and education.

Health

No matter what client group you coach, many of your clients will include health-related objectives in their list of goals. This is almost certainly a reflection of the times in which we live. Sixty years ago there were still people who believed that taking up smoking was beneficial to health. Now a majority of adult smokers believe they should give up smoking to improve and protect their health. Of course, it is a smaller subset of these people who actually want to give up smoking and an even smaller number who currently have the will to seriously try.

What motivates people to seek out help to give up smoking? There are a number of factors. These include:

- peer pressure
- the pester power of our children
- financial issues
- personal appearance and smell
- direct advice from health professionals
- experience of smoking-related poor health in ourselves or others.

In Paisley, Scotland, health coaching is offered to people aged 45–60 at risk of coronary heart disease and to people with established coronary heart disease who attend secondary prevention clinics. Health coaches use their skills to encourage people to adopt positive health behaviour changes, specifically in relation to the coronary heart disease risk factors of unhealthy eating, physical inactivity and tobacco use – and also to raise confidence and optimism to aid the change process.

(www.scotland.gov.uk/Publications/2006/11/29141927/7)

We do not know to what extent many of these factors are due to or boosted by the vigorous health education messages put out over many years. What we do know is that similar strategies are now being used to address a number of other behaviours that are considered to be damaging to the nation's health. These include:

- obesity and being overweight
- binge drinking and drinking during pregnancy
- lack of physical activity.

On top of this drive to change individual behaviours in order to drive up standards in the nation's health there is a new health-related issue in the headlines. This is the number of people who are out of work and in receipt of benefits on the grounds of poor health. There is good reason to believe that the numbers of ill-health related benefit claimants could be reduced radically if certain changes were made. These would include:

- Motivating employers to make adjustments to jobs and offer flexible working.

- Assessing people on what they are able to do rather than what they are not able to do.

- Motivating people on benefits to return to employment.

This is a new specialist interest area that looks set to mirror developments in the field of tackling long-term unemployment. In that field the public sector has joined forces with or awarded contacts to private companies to offer job search assistance, mentoring and coaching to long-term unemployed people.

If you have ambitious plans to grow a significant sized business which has the principles of coaching at the heart of its operations now is a really good time to investigate opportunities in the special interest area of 'health'. There are huge and growing opportunities in this special interest field.

Investors in People, an organisation dedicated to providing business improvement through people, has published a health and well-being at work resource pack aimed at helping people address health issues at work. One of its recommendations is that employers introduce personal lifestyle coaching to address individual lifestyle issues such as smoking, diet, exercise and sleeping.

(www.investorsinpeople.co.uk)

What do I need to build a business focusing on health issues?

Health professionals, by which I mean doctors, nurses and associated specially trained people such as dentists, physiotherapists, medical social workers, psychologists, occupational therapists, occupational health specialists and health visitors, all must receive specialist, usually degree and postgraduate level, training in order to work in their profession. For a variety of reasons, some very sound and some more open to debate, they and the people who employ them are often highly resistant to unqualified or differently qualified people working with clients who they think of as being in their care.

It will be a huge advantage to you in building a coaching business focusing on health issues if you or the coaches you deploy have some prior training/qualifications in a recognised health-related field. This may sound ridiculous to you. For example, if a GP's surgery wished to pilot a coaching programme designed to help patients lose weight, it seems obvious to a coach that the skills needed are coaching skills. But your GP will be thinking not only about outcomes but also about issues such as:

- patient health and safety
- insurance
- confidentiality.

He or she will know that a qualified health professional has received guidance on matters relating to confidentiality and client vulnerability. The GP practice manager will be confident that these bases will be covered without any extra work on his or her part and will already be working with insurers happy to cover the activities of qualified staff and sessional workers. When you roll up pitching for work with just your coaching qualifications, membership of a professional body and a list of references you might well be as alien to this potential client as an arrival from outer space.

This boils down to building trust. If you want to work in the special interest area of health you can build trust in the following ways.

- Hold or gain qualifications, or employ others with qualifications, that are recognised in health-related fields.

- Develop a track record of health-related work in a field where medical qualifications are not an essential. For example, attaching yourself to a slimmer's club or gym to help boost motivation.

- Volunteer your coaching skills to a voluntary sector organisation with a special focus on the health-related area in which you'd like to work (e.g. alcohol or drug dependency).

- Use existing business contacts to find work in the corporate sector. Many companies do have concerns about employee health. For example, some are under pressure from their permanent health insurers to gradually reintroduce people on long-term sick leave to the workplace. Your track record in management and general coaching will be of more relevance to this client group than any medical background.

If health matters interest you, this is likely to be a very rewarding area of focus for your business. By keeping an eye on the shifts in public policy you will find new areas to target and there is every indication that health-related coaching will remain a growing market for some time.

Sports

Sports coaching is concerned with both the development of technical skills and competence and the mental attitudes that will enable people to achieve their goals in sport. An excellent sports coach will be able to deliver in both of these areas. However, it is not at all unusual for elite and aspiring elite athletes to work with several different coaches. Each will focus on a specific aspect of the athlete's development, such as strength and conditioning, specific technical skill such as javelin throwing, and the psychological aspects.

Many universities now run degree and postgraduate degree courses in sports psychology. The leading governing bodies of sports employ or contract in psychologists and coaches specialising in the psychological aspects of athlete development to work with individual elite athletes or to advise on the development of policy and practice in a particular sport.

Given that sports coaching is becoming increasingly regulated in the UK, with recognised development pathways, accreditation processes and prescribed ways of working becoming the norm, is there room for you? Well, let's review the current situation as a way of answering that question.

Australian cricketer Glenn McGrath has been quoted as saying that over 60 per cent of 'talent' is down to mental strength.

- There are thousands of sports clubs in the UK ranging from a membership measured in single figures to over a 1000 people.

- Only a tiny percentage of athletes in the UK benefit from one-to-one sports coaching or free access to a sports psychologist to help their development.

- There are huge numbers of people participating in sport outside of the club network.

- There are national goals relating to participation and achievement in sport. Delivery agencies such as local authorities and sports governing bodies are not clear how they can or will deliver on these targets.

- 32,000 people finished the London Marathon in 2007. This is just one of hundreds of serious running events that tens of thousands of people train for in the UK every year.

- The UK has won two major sporting events – London 2012 and Glasgow 2014. Everyone involved in sport in the UK expects interest in sports participation and achievement to be boosted by these events.

Does this sound like a potential market that is not worth targeting? Every marathon runner wants to complete the marathon, many want to record a personal best, all of them have to motivate themselves to get out and run over weeks and weeks of training. Very few of them have a coach already. How do you make these sportspeople and others invest in your coaching skills?

> *Edinburgh and Scotland rugby player Scott Murray attributed the Scottish team's notable Six Nations victory over France in March 2008 as being due to a new positive mental attitude in the Scotland squad.*

There is no need to repeat what was stated in the previous section. The key to achieving a healthy number of clients in the special interest market of sports is in:

- building credibility – why not qualify as a sports coach and volunteer your time as you build your business?

Roehampton University's Sports Performance Assessment and Rehabilitation Centre promotes a service to runners seeking to develop a positive mental attitude. Its sports psychologists offer to help identify and develop an effective strategy to help runners stay focused on their goals throughout training and competition.
(www.roehampton.ac.uk/sparc/running/attitude/index.html)

- building trust – see above
- building experience – see above
- networking, using existing contacts and building new ones

Education

The moments at which we move into or out of education represent some of the most significant turning points in our lives. For school pupils and students there are a number of services that are free to the users and which are designed to dispense advice and guidance on further education, life and career choices. In theory these are wonderful, accessible services. In practice they are often under-funded, overstretched and extremely variable in quality.

Parents of children educated in the state sector are becoming used to recruiting and paying for additional tutorial support to help their children achieve a good standard of education. A small number are also beginning to see the value of investing in personally tailored support to help their offspring navigate effectively through the various transition points in their journey through education and into work.

Schools

The National College for School Leadership (NCSL) has issued several publications on the subject of coaching in schools. Its focus has been on the school leader who wants to embed coaching practices throughout a school. While the actual coaching it describes is coaching of teaching staff, it clearly aspires to see coaching style behaviour permeate entire schools. For example, the NCSL refers to the value of listening skills in classrooms and of tapping into people's passions and dreams to help make positive change happen.

When it comes to deploying coaching skills with pupils, behaviour management rather than individual achievement may be uppermost in the mind of a school head who takes an interest in coaching for his or her pupils. In recent times the language of coaching – the setting of goals and targets – has become familiar in schools. There is talk of individual learning plans for every pupil with goals set jointly between teaching staff and students so that each person reaches their full potential. Teachers are exhorted to find ways to motivate their pupils and some do manage this with excellent results.

Sadly, a number of factors combine to make it impossible for every school to live up to these ideals. Teacher skill and motivation is highly variable, class sizes can make individual attention an impossible dream and many students are not adequately supported at home. Repeated attempts by teaching unions to secure the resources needed to reduce class sizes has not persuaded central government to release enough resources to realise this goal. Not every school has an inspiring, strong leader who has managed to create a coaching style of leadership which positively influences the whole school. Some school leaders are struggling with ill, disaffected and incompetent teachers who are not easy to change or remove from their posts. All of this makes it likely that many of our children will experience poor quality teaching support at key moments in their school career.

According to the NCSL, school leaders have considered using a coaching style to:

- address pupil behaviour
- improve pupil performance
- build teams
- create a success culture
- grow the organisation
- develop assessment for learning
- improve the performance of teachers
- conduct the performance management of support staff
- develop lesson planning
- manage workforce reform
- deal with the negative influences of an individual
- spread good practice
- support a new head teacher
- create an inclusive school.

(www.ncsl.org.uk/media/883/AD/leading-coaching-in-schools.pdf).

Enter the 'new initiative' – a phrase likely to add to that sinking feeling so many teachers know only too well but one which might gladden the heart of any coach who dreams of inspiring young people.

Could you be the coach who introduces a new coaching initiative to your struggling school head? If you want to work with younger students and not just staff then you will need to comply fully with the rules on disclosure. Students under the age of 18 and vulnerable adults are offered special protection by law. Anyone working with them in a teaching role or engaging in unsupervised regular contact, for example, as a coach or tutor, should be subject to a full criminal records and background check. The exception is people recruited on a private basis by parents. In these private arrangements there is no legal requirement for a disclosure check to be carried out.

Further and higher education

Some coaches are beginning to work in association with further education colleges and universities to offer a coaching service for their students and recent graduates. Even if the institution is not prepared to subsidise this work through providing funding, it will often provide benefits in kind. These range from providing free office space for coaching sessions to promoting your service through internal and external communications and marketing exercises. This is a considerable potential benefit to your coaching enterprise and joint working with an educational institution should always be explored if this is a special market of interest to you.

Another benefit that association with an education institution confers on you is reputation by association. If a well-respected organisation promotes your service it is offering its tacit seal of approval. This can be worth a great deal when you seek other contracts in other or similar fields.

Coaching to get people into education or work

In a bid to build an economy based on an educated, skilled labour force the spotlight has focused in recent years on what some consider a worrying number of so-called NEETs. These are young people who are not in employment, education or training. The underlying assumption is that few of these people are failing to take up employment and education options for reasons that cannot be addressed.

Whether their exclusion from the worlds of work and education is self-imposed or the result of lack of skills, such as basic literacy, it is reasonable to suppose that they will need to find some source of motivation in order to change. Coaching style services, such as the support offered by organisations like Working Links (see box), are springing up to service this particular market. But there is an obvious challenge to developing a business which targets people who are not earning. Who pays for your services? The trick here is to work out who benefits. Who, apart from the unemployed youngster, is working to targets involving getting people back into work?

Working Links is an interesting organisation that takes a coaching style approach to enabling long-term unemployed people back into work. The organisation's aim is simple – to help as many people as they can overcome any barrier to enable them to get into paid work. The organisation was started by a bunch of like-minded people who wanted to help people without work. The organisation now operates out of more than 100 offices in the UK. Do you want to develop a business like this?

(www.workinglinks.co.uk)

The answer is the government and those organisations either contracted by the government to address this issue or which have an interest in supporting this potential client group.

If you have a background in education, training or careers advice you will already be pushing at an open door if you choose to enter this field. However, it is worth remembering that some of the most successful businesses operating in this sector today were started by people with just an idea that they could improve people's lives by helping them gain the confidence, motivation and skills to get into work.

5

Choosing the right client market

Deciding what the target markets for your business should be is a decision that must be based on a number of factors, including some good, solid research. When you take on all the risks of starting a new business you should never let your heart entirely rule your head. There are a lot of good reasons for taking time to decide what kind of people you want to attract as clients for your coaching business. These include:

- If you will be coaching, and not just managing other coaches, what type of people will you enjoy coaching?

- How much money must your business generate to meet your needs, and does the target market you have in mind have the ability to pay the fees you need to charge to make that money?

- Are you happy to work on attracting grant funding to your business or securing contracts with public sector organisations? This opens the door to working with disadvantaged groups such as young people not in employment, education or training who would be unlikely to afford the coaching fees themselves.

- Do you want to focus on telephone coaching or face to face? Most corporate coaching work involves high levels of face-to-face coaching.

Welcome to Coaching Mums!

Do you ever say to yourself?

■ *'There must be something more than this!'*
■ *'I'd love to do something for me for a change!'*
■ *'What happened to the confident woman I used to be whose world was her oyster?'*

Our purpose at Coaching Mums is to help women like you to put the wind back in your sails, set course for your dream destination, and to thoroughly enjoy the journey.

(www.coachingmums.co.uk)

■ Is there a gap in the market? Is there a target market that other coaches have overlooked which you could capture?

■ Do you have contacts which could give you a head start in a particular market? Coaching business plans I have seen include one targeting women returning to work after having children, one targeting people coming up for retirement and one targeting NHS staff seeking a career change. In each case the coach had direct experience of the needs of their target market and contact with the target group either directly or through contacts in large organisations.

You could spend 30+ years in retirement – more than any other stage of your life...

You've worked hard to achieve an 'ideal' retirement lifestyle, but what does that really mean to you?

Retirement planning isn't just financial planning – an important factor – but also HOW you can create an enjoyable and enriching retirement life.

(www.retirementcoach.co.uk)

Lots of people putting together a coaching business plan decide to say that they will coach everyone. There is absolutely nothing wrong with offering coaching to anyone who approaches your business as long as they are in a fit state to benefit from your skills. So why is this chapter all about identifying your 'target markets'? Well take a look at the boxes dotted about these pages and next. Each of these is a short extract from the websites of coaching businesses. Each targets a particular group. Why do you think other coaches are being so specific in their marketing messages?

The coaches advertising here know exactly what type of clients they want to attract to their business. We do not know why they chose these groups, or even if they actually do draw most of their clients from these groups of people. But if we think about the three groups being appealed to by these coaches we can start to

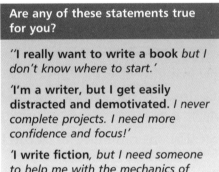

Are any of these statements true for you?

"I really want to write a book *but I don't know where to start.'*

'I'm a writer, but I get easily distracted and demotivated. *I never complete projects. I need more confidence and focus!'*

'I write fiction, *but I need someone to help me with the mechanics of characterisation, plotting and structuring my novel.'*

(www.thewritingcoach.co.uk)

work out the advantages of sending out a message which is so clearly targeted at a clearly defined social group.

These coaches are appealing to:

- mothers with children under 18
- people about to retire
- writers and would-be writers.

For all we know the founders of these businesses may have based their decision to target these groups simply because working with such people is a source of real joy to them. But whatever their reasons for choosing these groups they will certainly have derived many benefits from targeting these groups so clearly.

PEOPLE LIKE PEOPLE LIKE THEMSELVES

Whoever first said that opposites attract must not have been looking at the overwhelming evidence to the contrary. Equal opportunity and anti-discrimination campaigners are still struggling to reduce the rate of people recruiting to jobs in their own image. In 2007, the Norwegian Government passed a law requiring companies to meet a non-negotiable quota specifying how many women they must have on the board. The reason for this draconian action was the glacial pace of voluntary change which saw men recruiting more men and ensuring that their organisations continued to be run by people just like them.

Take a look at your own friendship group. How many of your friends are from completely different ethnic, class, religious backgrounds from you? How many earn a vastly different income to yours, do radically different work or live their daily lives very differently from how you live yours?

Whether you think this clustering together of like-minded, culturally similar people is good or bad is not the point. As a business person you can make it work to your advantage. This is because:

People talk

If someone has a good experience of being coached by you they will tell their friends and colleagues about it. This generates referrals, the lifeblood of any coaching business. When people see each other frequently they will always find time to chat. Informal, word-of-mouth recommendations are the stuff of gold to new businesses. Satisfied clients will spread the word about your excellent coaching service. So, if you want to rapidly build your business choose people who tend to have good levels of social contact.

And let's not forget that:

Targeted advertising works

In these days of fast-forwarding and time-shifting viewing of favourite programmes, the television industry is finding it hard to convince advertisers that an investment in television advertising is worthwhile. But even though the glory days of television advertising appear to be over you will see the concept of audience targeting at work on contemporary television.

Have you ever seen an advertisement for stair lifts or denture fixatives in the middle of a post-watershed television drama which 'contains scenes of a sexually explicit nature and swearing'? I doubt it. But tune into Channel 4's longstanding word game *Countdown* one afternoon and that's what you will see in the advertisement breaks. Obviously not everyone who watches *Countdown* is frail, elderly and toothless but judging by the appearance of the studio audience this is certainly a programme that appeals to the over-65s. The stair lift company chooses breaks during Channel 4's afternoon show *Countdown* because their research tells them that a significant number of people watching this programme will be interested in or badly in need of its lifts.

Knowing your target market and its habits helps you decide where to advertise and how best to promote your service. This saves time and money because you need to take fewer actions and use up fewer resources if you can reach a lot of people via a limited number of routes. So if you are going to make your business successful then some serious consideration has to go to targeting the right client market.

Identifying your target market

Take a look at the following list. Which types of people would tend to have frequent social and/or professional contact with other people in a similar position to themselves?

- a frail elderly widowed pensioner
- a busy mother, the chair of the PTA, who picks her kids up from school every day
- a local authority employee coming up for retirement
- an unemployed 22-year-old with mild depression
- a would-be novelist
- a senior manager in a large financial institution.

Now ask yourself:

- Where would they meet these similar people?
- Would they be likely to be the sort of person who influences others?

Now look at the list again.

- Which of these people would be most likely to be able to afford a series of coaching sessions with you?

Now study the list from another perspective:

- Who isn't being clearly targeted by your competitors?

If you already know that you don't want to work with any of these types of people then who do you want to work with? Doctors, frustrated singers, young people leaving university, first jobbers looking at next step options or what about professional sportspeople retiring as a result of age or injury? When you know, write it down and keep looking at the potential of this group of people from every angle. Remember, whatever your personal goals, everyone running a coaching business needs a target group that will bring them:

- job satisfaction
- referrals
- enough money to keep running the business they love.

THE GREAT DIVIDE: CORPORATE VS PERSONAL

One of the biggies in coaching is a perceived divide between corporate and personal coaching. While the former is an increasingly well-respected and widely invested in field, the latter, often known as the 'life coaching' market is much less easy to research and analyse, and is still regarded with a deal of suspicion by many people. Criticisms levelled at life coaching include the suggestion that it is too American for British people, that it is an industry riddled with under-qualified, incompetent practitioners, an indulgence for rich, bored and dim people, and a passing fad of no real use to sensible people.

In reality, there are too many incompetent practitioners trading as life coaches and sensible people can often transform their own lives and solve their own problems without going anywhere near a coach. A few of my clients have seemed a little under-motivated and over-resourced for me to feel entirely convinced of their commitment to the coaching process.

Many coaches work in both fields and many specialise in one or the other. If you look at a number of coaching websites you will see that lots of organisations that offer coaching, large and small, try to tailor their messages to these two different markets by having separate pages for each of them. Just do a Google search on 'coaching services' and you will see how many of your competitors appear to be successfully straddling the great divide.

This chapter is about identifying your target markets – yes, you can target more than one market. It is perfectly fine to go after several different markets as other successful coaches demonstrate. What is not OK is projecting an image and creating an impression that is very right for one of your target markets and very wrong for another. Avoiding this creates an elephant trap. Once you start trying to appeal to several groups you are at risk of putting out bland, confusing messages that appeal to no one or, at least, don't appeal enough to anyone. It is a trap best avoided. This is why I would urge those of you setting up in business on a small-scale as a sole trader to aim for the following:

- Identify and research one target client group.

- Market your service effectively to them.

- When this is accomplished and you are successfully working with the type of clients you wanted to recruit, move on to identifying, researching and targeting your next client group.

The only sensible exception to this is if your targeting/marketing processes fail. If the group you targeted and the techniques used failed to generate sufficient numbers of paying clients, then you must do some more research rapidly. Try again by changing your marketing activities and set yourself a time limit for starting to work on your next client group.

The special benefits of working in corporate coaching

If charging relatively high rates for your coaching work and achieving substantial levels of repeat business are important factors in your business plan, then you cannot afford to turn your back on corporate coaching. If you don't like dressing smartly in classic business gear, working face to face with your clients or working for paymasters that sometimes want you involved just to 'move people on' to pastures new, then corporate coaching isn't for you.

There are several important benefits of working in the corporate sector. Once an organisation has experienced the benefit of your coaching it will want to use you again. Large organisations have significant staff churn (i.e. turnover) and HR managers are engaged in an ongoing process of ensuring staff learning and development is moving forwards. The benefits of working in corporate coaching include:

■ One contact (e.g. a head of HR) can generate hundreds of referrals.

■ Coaches are often seen as helping to solve 'difficult cases'. When you solve a manager's problem by, for example, enabling a bored middle manager to move on to pastures new, they are very grateful to you. Gratitude is often repaid by finding more work for you.

■ Senior managers meet with others outside their organisation. One word of recommendation from them can open up a huge new market.

■ When staff you have coached get that promotion or that new job they will remember that you helped them and maybe want to bring you in to work with their new team. That's potentially another big organisation opened up to you.

- Fees are generally higher than in the personal/life coaching sector.

The flexibility of personal coaching

What are your target markets?

Who will you coach and why?
Remember that:

- *Inspiring coaches need to feel energised by their clients.*
- *You have to believe in your client's willingness to change.*
- *You have to be able to build rapport with your clients.*
Do you need to rethink your target group with these facts in mind?

Lots of people choose personal coaching because they can take on a few clients, working with them in the evenings and at weekends while keeping the day job. Then, when they start to develop their business they are disconcerted to find that the target market they chose still wants to book evening and weekend sessions. Suddenly they realise that switching over to coaching as their main income and delivering on their business plan appears to require a lot of evening and weekend working. They now know for a fact that they don't like working at evenings and weekends and so their plan threatens to deliver them a working life they really don't want.

Be warned, this is a very common pitfall for people working in personal and life coaching who choose to build up their business slowly while sticking at the day job. It is not inevitable but it can be a consequence of choices you make when you are deciding your target market. A successful coach can tough this one out. As a highly successful therapist once told me, even a factory worker tied to the production line will make an 11 am session right in the middle of his shift if he really thinks the therapy will help. But this approach takes confidence, a high-profile in the industry and a glowing reputation. Beginners rarely have this.

If you want to stick to mainly daytime, weekday working make it easy on yourself. Consider client groups that can work with you on week days. These include:

- people who work in the home whose children are at school
- students
- retired people
- part-time workers
- senior managers who can obtain privacy at work to call you
- people trying to get back into employment, for example, following ill health
- teachers who can call after 4 pm or during holidays.

If you choose to target young ambitious professionals many will argue that their pressurised jobs prohibit taking time out to call you. Don't despair. Using your coaching skills you might be able to get them to set some goals around making time by better organising their workload or calling you earlier than they would find ideal.

Above all, when choosing a target client group, use coaching techniques on yourself. When you uncover a potential problem, for example, this problem of a target client group's availability not matching with your preferences, apply the question you should always ask clients who have become stuck because they cannot see how they can overcome barriers. That question is: What other options are there which would get you what you want?

6

How Will You Deliver Your Coaching?

There are two main modes of delivering an effective coaching service. These are face to face and telephone. As the technology becomes more accessible, coaches are also offering web-based coaching. The affordability of on-line communication methods makes this an increasingly interesting option. A fast broadband Internet connection, a reasonably new computer and a cheap microphone and webcam (both often built-in to new machines) and some free and easily downloadable software are all you need to achieve any or all of the following options:

- Coaching by email.
- Coaching by instant messaging.
- Coaching 'face to face', using a camera.

There are advantages and disadvantages to using each of these methods for coaching. The best possible coaching service would offer a mix of methods. However, this has implications for your investment of time and money in your business. For example, the greater your reliance on IT systems to deliver your coaching, the more important it will be to invest in IT support services that will enable you to fix computer or broadband connection problems quickly. Opting for face-to-face coaching is the low-tech option and the dominant mode of coaching when working with corporate clients. This is particularly true of running a coaching service targeting senior managers. However, the travel time involved and the limit it places on the number of clients you can coach in a day has to be considered when you plan your pricing structure.

THINKING ABOUT YOUR MODES OF COACHING

The main elements to consider when planning what modes of coaching to offer are:

- How do you want to work? Do you prefer coaching face to face? Do you like being mainly home based?

- Is there a tradition or culture of coaching in the field in which you want to work which demands you offer certain modes of coaching?

- Can you create a competitive advantage by offering a variety of modes of coaching?

- Is the mode of coaching you want to prioritise suitable for your target clients?

The following information summarises advantages and disadvantages of each mode of coaching to help you shape your coaching service.

FACE-TO-FACE COACHING

If you prefer to work in your pyjamas, telephone headset nestled in your bedhead hair, pacing about your home office while listening intently to your clients, face-to-face coaching might not be for you. But what might you be missing out on if you choose not to work face to face?

Body language

Not all your clients will have a face that could launch a 1000 ships but it is true that every picture tells a story. Face-to-face coaching allows you to observe what your client's body tells you about their mood, thoughts and feelings. That jiggling leg might signify frustration or impatience, those folded arms could be a sign that you have asked a question that comes close to an issue they find it difficult to discuss.

NLP

Coaches who decide to train in NLP skills will often prefer to work face to face because of the opportunity to deploy a skill which they refer to as 'calibration'. NLP is short for neuro-linguistic programming. Fans of NLP will say that all coaches need to learn how to become NLP practitioners because this is the route to becoming an excellent coach. Some deride the field of NLP for being an over-hyped, over-complicated way of doing what all good coaches do – which is to listen to and observe their clients closely in order to better understand how best to help them move forward and make the right choices for them.

In the world of NLP, 'calibration' means simply that the coach is tuning in to their clients feelings by accurately reading non-verbal signals. These can be aural signals. For example, the way in which a person's voice tone changes when they are on the brink of tears or their pace of speech quickens as they speak of something they would rather not focus on. But many of the signs are visual. The way a client furrows their brow when they speak of something they admit they are unhappy about might be repeated when they talk, apparently neutrally, about another part of their life. Once they had noted certain gestures and expressions as being linked to certain emotions, the NLP practitioner would say they had 'calibrated' their client. From then on they might be able to ask more incisive questions by noting a gesture that indicates a particular feeling and surprising the clients with their intuitiveness.

Whether you buy into NLP and all its associated theories, it is clear that listening is only one aspect of 'reading' your client. Meeting their needs by asking truly powerful questions will sometimes be far easier when you are working face to face because of all the non-verbal clues on offer.

Building rapport

Building rapport can also sometimes be easier when working face to face. You too can offer non-verbal clues to your client, positive and negative. These non-verbal messages can help put your client at ease and build mutual trust more rapidly than is possible when you are limited by the constraints of telephone coaching. For example, dressing professionally in a way that mirrors the dress of a corporate client is likely to help them feel that you will be on the same wavelength as them. If you then start mirroring their gestures, as people do naturally when they like each other and are getting along well, you will build further rapport.

This non-verbal aspect of coaching is a two-way street. While it can be a huge advantage to observe your client, remember that you too will be observed. Let's start with that old favourite – first impressions. Get your style of dress wrong, arrive wild-eyed and sweaty, having sprinted from a faraway parking place and up three flights of stairs or looking like you are still having that row about the last night's washing-up which gave you such a bad start to the day, and you'll be taking at least three steps back on the rapport building front.

Every non-verbal signal you give out can be read by your clients. Deliberate mirroring, which can work so well to build rapport, has to be conducted with great subtlety. You should take it easy. If they lean towards you, you can afford to do likewise. If they flail their arms around dramatically to make a particular point and you mirror that you risk creating the impression that you are playing a one-sided game of 'Simple Simon Says'.

Do your clients sometimes bore you? Annoy you? Frustrate you? Are you expert at keeping your body language under control? If not, then they will pick up on your inner thoughts and feelings. All effective coaching requires high levels of self-control in the coach, never more so than when that coaching is conducted face to face.

Face to face dominates in business and executive coaching

Executive coaching, the coaching of managers at senior and board level, is the top end of business coaching. Busy people tend to opt for services that are delivered to them and tend to have the money to pay for personally tailored services. Middle managers, if they have ambition and any sense, will tend to mirror the behaviour of those on the higher rungs of the corporate ladder. Perhaps this is why the dominant mode of delivering coaching in the corporate sector has tended to be face to face.

There are drawbacks to this model. Firstly, top managers often have their own offices and will invite you into their territory to be coached. In fact a neutral space is better for coaching. Managers can find it hard to relax and be open in an environment where the opposite mode of behaviour has become the norm. This means that coaching in this market poses two main challenges:

1   Finding affordable, appropriate space for the coaching sessions
2   Travelling to meet clients.

There are cost implications here. Busy people will not want to travel great distances for their coaching and so it is unlikely that you will be able to conduct client sessions in your own office space. Your travel time has to be factored into your fee structure. It is not unrealistic to assume that a single 45-minute to 1-hour coaching session will consume half a day of your time – often more. Don't be afraid to consider a fee structure that prices one executive coaching session at a similar rate to what you might aim to earn in a full day's worth of telephone coaching.

CASE STUDY: LITTLE GIRL LOST

Lorna was frustrated by her lack of progress up her organisation's career ladder. She felt she was stuck in a junior manager's post. She knew she was filling in application forms correctly because she always secured an interview. Her annual performance reviews were always glowing. She had asked for feedback after unsuccessful interviews but she felt people were not telling her what she really needed to know.

Coaching Lorna face to face proved to be almost an instant key to unravelling the mystery of her lack of success. The organisation had recently undergone a review. Everyone knew that it was trying to shake off an image of having fallen somewhat behind the times. Lorna was a smartly dressed woman but her good quality clothes were years out of date. She was also a small woman.

At her first session she perched on her chair nervously, feet swinging clear of the floor and she frequently placed her hand over her mouth, sucked her hair or sucked a finger when asked questions which caused her to feel uncomfortable. The overall impression she created was of a lost little girl and yet the jobs she was seeking demanded a candidate who acted with authority and displayed leadership. She also had a habit of pursing her lips when she spoke about anything of which she disapproved. This expression flickered into action whenever she talked about any of the managers already on the team she was trying so hard to join, even when she appeared to be talking enthusiastically about a new job vacancy she hoped to target.

Having noted the non-verbal clues which included her dress, her childish body language and her pursed lips which often undermined what she was saying, her coach was able to quickly draw Lorna's attention to the gap between how she thought of herself and how others were likely to perceive her.

After two sessions Lorna went shopping for new work clothes, after the third she decided to look outside the organisation for her next job. Following some specific coaching on interview technique, Lorna is now working in the same organisation a good step up the management ladder.

TELEPHONE COACHING

Having championed the wonders of tuning into non-verbal signals during face-to-face coaching you might feel that I am about to deride telephone coaching as a second-rate mode of delivering your business. Far from it. Telephone coaching can be incredibly effective and can even be the best mode of coaching for some people.

Anyone who is shy, who feels judged on their appearance or who has serious financial or physical constraints which might otherwise prevent them from accessing coaching might miss out on coaching altogether if the only option is to see their coach face to face. For some people, the intimacy of a private phone call allows them to relax and be more open and honest more quickly than they would manage when talking face to face. If you think you need to take care in choosing your clothes for a face-to-face session think about what your clients might be going through. There is something potentially very relaxing for some people about being heard but not seen.

Benefits of telephone coaching

There are also benefits to you as a coach. For the dedicated home worker or the remote rural-based coach, the phone puts you in touch with clients anywhere and at any time that suits you both. You can pride yourself on reducing your carbon emissions and increasing your leisure time by cutting travel from your weekly workload. You can fit in more sessions per day because little time is needed between sessions. In fact, the only constraints on numbers of clients are your own energy levels and client availability. Costs are cut significantly for the telephone coach. You can make a positive impression without investing in smart work clothes, a smart office or a car. Your travel budget will be minimal and even your phone bill will be modest as it is common practice for clients to call you.

But can you take pride in working as effectively as you might in face-to-face coaching sessions? The answer lies with you and with your choice of clients. I am personally happy to work both ways and do not feel that quality is noticeably impaired by cutting out visual signals. However, I am a very speech-focused person. For example, in daily life I often find it easier to recognise voices than faces. I listen to radio a lot and even when working face to face with clients I have often found myself responding more to how someone sounds than to what I have seen.

I am also more in control of my environment when waiting for an incoming call from a client than I am when I visit clients at their place of work. I can be on my own; I can take time to gather my thoughts without distractions and to entirely focus on the client, perhaps by reading notes from a previous session. This focusing makes for a more productive session in my experience.

Additionally, I think some clients can focus more on themselves if they are not distracted by me. What I look like, what I convey through other non-verbal signals can be distracting for clients. While telephone coaching can require longer, more self-conscious efforts to build rapport, once established I think it is harder to damage rapport in telephone coaching. If you forget to place your watch or a clock where both you and the client can see it in a face-to-face session you will be forced to check the time in order to gauge when to end the session. A sly glance at your watch might be all it takes for your client to jump to the conclusion that you have lost interest in them. Their rational thoughts might agree with you, they know the session has to run to time but their emotions might lead them to feel uncomfortable. Just one look – that's all it sometimes takes to damage rapport.

Finally, there is the convenience of telephone coaching, not just to you but to your clients. It is increasingly common for business coaching to include a mix of face-to-face and telephone coaching. People who travel for their work find it hard to make regular appointments for meetings and need the flexibility of long-distance communication tools.

Telephone coaching is not a second class form of coaching. Like any tool it should be used only when appropriate.

Coaching by email

Many coaches now offer email support between coaching sessions. This can range from sending an immediate summary of goals set and actions agreed in a session to conducting coaching 'conversations' entirely by email.

Email is a great tool for communicating quickly and cheaply with clients. It is not a great tool for use as a primary mode of coaching. Apart from the obvious drawbacks of offering no visual or aural contact with your client, an email can be the product of endless edits. There is a huge value in hearing or seeing your client's front of mind response. Picking up on their first response, rather than their carefully considered answer, to your questions can be hugely instructive. It helps you to know what their heart says, not just their head. And it helps them to have you pick up quickly on inconsistencies, hesitations, turns of phrase and other clues to their actual feelings, ideas, hopes, fears and general state of mind. The inevitable time delay between sending an email and receiving a response and the ability to edit one's responses in an email can severely undermine a coach's ability to coach effectively.

Using email as a means of managing communications between

you and your clients between sessions is helpful. Using it as a substitute for some form of real time contact with your clients is not a good idea.

There is one other serious pitfall which emails between coach and client can lead to. Clients do sometimes benefit from the shot of confidence that a timely 'well done' from their coach can deliver. It would appear that if they email you between sessions to report progress and you email back a positive response there can be no harm done. But what if they email to secure your agreement to a variation in goals set or to explain a setback or change of mind? How should you handle this? A busy coach may not have time to respond appropriately, a wise coach will not want to start encouraging this type of deviation from an agreed course of action between sessions. If you do use email between sessions take care that you do not fall into a trap of undermining the progress your client agrees to make in each actual coaching session.

Coaching by instant messaging

Unlike email, there does not need to be any significant time delay between one person typing in a question and the other responding. Instant messaging services such as those provided by MSN (www.msn.com), Yahoo (www.yahoo.com) and Skype (www.skype.com) allow you to have a written online conversation in real time. If your client starts editing his or her responses then you will notice some delay. You won't, of course, find out what caused the delay unless you ask them. They might just be thinking carefully before they answer a powerful question.

Instant messaging is, like email, obviously limiting for anyone who finds expressing themselves through writing challenging. It also deprives you of visual and aural clues to your client's state of mind. Any written form of communication makes it harder for you to build and maintain rapport. Your questions, which while remaining powerful, can be rendered less abrupt or sound less challenging by subtle shifts in your timing and tone of voice, will seem quite demanding in written form. In British culture we often try to soften written requests and demands by over-writing – adding all sorts of words and additional phrases to make our request seem more polite and acceptable. For example, 'I wonder if you could return this to me...' instead of 'When will you send it back?', or 'Would it be possible to consider asking...' Instead of 'When will you ask...'.

There must be a reason for this hesitancy to indulge in plain speaking when writing to someone. If you are afraid of offending your clients by delivering your powerful questions in writing just as you would in speech take care. There is no point swapping plain speaking for blurry writing. You clients deserve the very best support whatever mode of communication you use.

For these reasons I wouldn't enter into coaching by text. Nt 4 enny uvva reeson cept I cnt gt wht people meen.

Coaching via webcam

Nowadays, anyone with a fast-enough broadband connection and a computer which allows you to easily connect to, or which has, a built-in webcam and microphone can see the face and hear the voice of their client even if they are on different continents.

Skype (www.skype.com) is a free communications tool which can be downloaded onto your computer. You can use it, and other systems such as MSN's messaging systems (www.msn.com), to conduct instant text messaging, voice and video messaging with others who subscribe to the same service. Voice message conversations via services such as Skype are usually free.

Suddenly you have the capacity to see your client as well as to hear them without being in the same room. Does this offer an effective mode of coaching which bridges the gap between the travel and time demands of face-to-face coaching work and the drawbacks of never actually meeting your clients because you do all your coaching by phone? It does not quite achieve this for me but this may be due to my discomfort with the technology rather than an actual problem inherent in the system.

Usually on television news you will see webcam-style live broadcasts used to provide live reports from far-flung places and there is always some delay which separates image and voice. This can be very off-putting and, for me, totally undermines one of the main benefits of seeing your client which is being able to link non-verbal, mainly visual clues with the words they are saying. The technology is constantly improving though. If I am to be honest, the drawback for me is that I am unable to sit in front of a webcam without feeling self-conscious. I am distracted both by the tendency to keep worrying that I might look odd to my client and by the possibility that the technology might be as distracting to them as it is to me. I have also had such connections fail, inexplicably, at the last minute. While a simple redial of a phone number has served me well in 99 per cent of problem phone calls (except when someone severed my main phone line while installing our new drive – but that's hardly a regular occupational hazard), I have often failed to fix a broken voice-to-voice or webcam link. This is really bad news for you and your client. It is often impossible to reschedule sessions quickly if you have a busy caseload.

So, if you do want to use this technology:

■ consider how you will access adequate support for your IT systems

■ always have a normal phone number to contact as back-up to enable you to complete interrupted sessions

■ make sure your naked dancing partner doesn't wobble into the room while you are online (see I told you I wasn't comfortable with the technology).

A word about mobile phones

It may seem incredible to some of you but some people no longer have any phone but a mobile phone. Does this matter? Well, it will affect your profits if you end up calling them for a coaching session. An hour's coaching can cost nothing at all if your have the right phone deal and call from landline to landline at the right time of day. The cost could exceed the fee your client is paying if you have the wrong phone deal and call a mobile number at peak time either from your landline or from a mobile on a different network to that of your clients.

And if you can fix the cost problem? I try to avoid the double trouble of mobile-to-mobile coaching. Signal strengths vary and the risks of being cut off are still far higher on mobile-to-mobile calls than on landlines. Then, there is the risk of distraction and interruption. I will not coach clients who are obviously on the move or calling from a public place. This is just because the attention they can give to the session is always limited if they are not speaking from a quiet, private, undisturbed space. A coaching conversation conducted on the move, from a busy office or restaurant or on a phone afflicted by fading battery power (yes, I have had clients try all of these) is not likely to result in the best possible outcomes for your client and that is why I try to avoid using mobile phones.

I do use them to fix appointments and have actively encouraged clients to use my mobile number if they need to reschedule an appointment. It is helpful to both coach and client if these matters can be resolved quickly.

7

Form Follows Function – Designing Your Business Structure

Most coaching businesses start on a part-time basis while the coach carries out other work which might be paid or unpaid. I received my first coaching training as part of a programme of management training and started using coaching skills with people I managed. I also coached people in the organisation which employed me who were looking to develop their career. Others seek out coaching training as a deliberate step towards changing careers or moving back into work after time spent raising a family or for some other reason.

My first experience of coaching was as an employee. I did not have to find clients in order to make my living – I was a salaried member of staff who could take time to coach others when demand was there. I very much enjoyed this part-time, relatively stress-free coaching role. When I started considering coaching as a career option I was clear that coaching full-time would not be suitable for me. I was also clear that I did not want to dedicate my time to setting up a large, successful coaching business which employed lots of other people. How did I know this? Well, by that time I had worked in lots of different roles and had a pretty good idea of my strengths and weaknesses. I also knew what types and what patterns of work motivated me to work hard and enabled me to feel proud of my achievements. I also knew a lot about the areas of work I particularly disliked.

For example, my true passion is not coaching. I enjoy coaching immensely. I find it challenging and rewarding. This does not alter the fact that one of my real work passions is writing. I knew that coaching full-time or employing other coaches to build a full-time coaching business would not help me spend more time doing the work I enjoy best. This book is a product of my passion for communicating in writing. I also knew something else about myself – I enjoy team working and working with groups too much to give it up completely. There is not too much team work in the business of writing and coaching is always most effective on a one-to-one basis. So, my business strategy has been to focus on using coaching skills mainly in the context of delivering training courses. This allows me to work with others but does not require me to take on the full responsibility of running a business which employs other people. I have been happy to start my business as a self-employed person who does not plan to employ other people. I sometimes work with others in one-off project-specific partnerships and I sometimes also work part-time as an employee (rather than a consultant or contractor) for other organisations.

This works for me because I know that coaching full-time or building a large, successful coaching business which employs lots of people was never my goal. But what will work for you? What business structure will help you meet your personal and your business goals? What follows are some classic options for organising your coaching business. There are also some diagnostic exercises to help you better understand what will work best for you.

BECOMING A SOLE TRADER

In the UK, a sole trader must be registered with HM Revenue and Customs for tax and national insurance purposes. You can register online, by phone or by post, and there is excellent advice available at the government's website (www.hmrc.gov.uk/startingup/reg ister.htm).

Being a sole trader does not mean that you cannot employ other people or work with others in casual or temporary partnerships. You can remain a sole trader while being sub-contracted by others to carry out specific pieces of work which place you in a team working together. You can also be a part-time sole trader while working full- or part-time for others. The main issue here is that your earnings as a sole trader (i.e. your self-employed earnings) must be accounted for separately from your earnings derived from employment. This is partly due to rules around taxation. When you are employed, your tax and national insurance will be deducted by your employer before you receive your pay by means of the Pay As You Earn (PAYE) system. As a sole trader you will be responsible for declaring your earnings from self-employment and saving money to pay a tax bill twice a year and to pay your NI contributions.

The basics of working as a sole trader

Becoming a sole trader is a simple process which does not require you to register anywhere except with HM Revenue and Customs. It can be an ideal way to start a part-time business but there are some drawbacks. These downsides usually only become apparent when you consider employing other people or expanding your business in ways which require significant borrowing or taking on other potentially costly liabilities. This is because as a sole trader you have complete responsibility for every aspect of the business. You cannot separate your business finances from your personal finances. It is good practice to separate them in principle by running separate business and personal bank accounts. This helps clarify financial matters for tax purposes. However, in law, a sole trader cannot separate personal and business finances. This means that as a sole trader you have unlimited personal liability. You are personally responsible for any liabilities caused by the business.

What does this mean in practice? Well, imagine you did not take out public liability insurance and one of your clients slipped on a pen you had left on the floor of the room in which you coach. What if their injury led to their requiring a major operation on their knee and they decided to make a claim against you for the cost of their treatment, their loss of earnings and their mental distress? If your business does not have tens of thousands of pounds saved up to cover such an eventuality, then if the claimant is successful, your personal savings will be chased down next, and if that isn't enough there could be a case for forcing you to release equity in your home to meet the cost of their legal action against you.

Remember – a sole trader must:

- pay income tax on the profits made by the business and account for all the financial dealings of the business

- accept sole liability for all and unlimited debts and obligations.

Don't panic! With the right insurances in place, a good accountant recruited and/or excellent record-keeping in place, a low-risk occupation such as coaching should not lead you into difficulties.

But be warned. The freedom implied by being your own boss in the light touch, largely unregulated world of sole trading may come with a hidden price tag. The upside is that a sole trader will:

■ be able to make every decision that affects the business without consulting others if they choose

■ manage and own all the assets of the business.

Benefits of working as a sole trader

The benefits of working as a sole trader are mainly the relatively low time and money costs of setting up and running your business in this way. I would always advise contracting an accountant to help you keep excellent financial records and submit an accurate tax return each year, but a sole trader is not required to employ an accountant. There is no requirement to report on your annual finances to anyone other than HM Revenue and Customs and no required format to record your business finances other than by completing the appropriate tax return. Very small coaching practices with low incomes will not even be required to complete a full tax return (providing that other aspects of your personal finances do not already require a full tax return from you each year).

Similarly, there is no requirement to contract a legally qualified person to help constitute or in any other way create your business. There are no legal documents required to show that you are working as a sole trader which makes this an appealing way to start out.

If your business will trade under a name different to your own name you must take certain steps to ensure that the name chosen is appropriate and available for use. Advice on this is contained in Chapter 8.

FORMING A PARTNERSHIP

Partnerships: liability for debts

In England, Northern Ireland and Wales partners are jointly liable for paying off debts. This means they are equally responsible for paying all the money owed by the partnership. They are not severally liable. This would mean that each member of the partnership was responsible for paying the whole debt. In Scotland partners are both jointly and severally liable.

There are several different ways of forming a partnership. At its most simple, a partnership business is one formed by the making of a simple agreement between one or more people. It does not need to be anchored by a written contract or overseen by a lawyer or accountant however advisable it might be to do so. This form of simple partnership, usually known as a general partnership, is then subject to all the same liabilities as a sole trader. The only difference is that these liabilities are shared equally among the partners. Each partner must register as self-employed and the partnership must be dissolved if any partner is lost – whether to death, resignation or bankruptcy. The business can continue to trade even if the partnership is dissolved. This is because the partnership is not the business. The partnership is simply an agreed way of running the business.

This might sound like a great idea. After all, a burden shared is a burden halved. Now think about the concept of 'double trouble'. Your liabilities are shared in a partnership but so too are the responsibilities. This is when it becomes obvious that it is advisable to define partnerships by means of a written, legally binding partnership agreement. A business can become paralysed very quickly when two or more partners cannot agree on a course of action. It could be something as simple as the design of a promotional leaflet or investment in a new broadband connection. If you cannot agree then it is hard to move forward.

Having said that, a simple business needs only a simple partnership agreement to help secure a way round potential obstacles. I worked happily for some time with two fellow journalists running a small news agency. We were bound together by shared experience (we had worked on the same magazine team), a shared vision for our small business and carefully drawn-up agreements which defined roles and responsibilities, decision-making processes and what would happen to profits plus what would happen to assets if the business ceased to trade. We obtained legal advice and signed a general partnership agreement.

There is also the option of a limited liability partnership. This type of partnership is not very different from a general partnership. Again all the partners are self-employed and they have overall responsibility for the whole of the business. However, in a limited liability partnership, liability is limited to the amount that each partner invested in the business and/or to any guarantees they offered in the course of securing investment/finance for the business.

The advantage of a limited liability partnership is that each partner enjoys some protection from financial ruin if the business runs into difficulties. However, not all partners are equal in such a partnership. The law requires that at least two partners must become 'designated partners' and these partners have additional responsibilities placed upon them. It is also a requirement that such partnerships register at Companies House.

For full information on setting up a limited liability partnership you can log onto the Companies House website at www.companies house.gov.uk.

To search for a solicitor or accountant to advise you go to the Law Society or Institute of Chartered Accountants websites (www.law society.org.uk; www.icaewfirms.co.uk).

BECOMING A LIMITED COMPANY

There are two main different types of limited liability companies. These are:

1   private limited companies
2   public limited companies (plcs).

The rule governing how companies must be set up and the legal requirements placed on running companies have changed in recent years. The relevant laws are contained in the 2006 Companies Act. Guidance on the detail of the Act is available from Companies House (www.companieshouse.gov.uk). You can also get good advice from professionally qualified people such as accountants and lawyers specialising in this area. Make sure you do. It is easy to break the law by operating your business as a company but failing to observe all the rules. For example, companies have long been required to display their company number and registered business address on all letters. Now these rules apply also to electronic communications.

Main differences between private limited companies and plcs

There are several important differences between private and public limited companies. For example, private limited companies cannot issue shares to the public but can have more than one shareholder. Public limited companies must have at least two shareholders and must have issued shares to the public to the value of at least £50,000 before they can trade.

Both types of company must register at Companies House and file their accounts there by a specific deadline each year. These accounts must be audited. Private limited companies must have at least one director who is aged 16 or over. Plcs must have at least two directors and may be required to appoint a qualified company secretary and notify this to Companies House. Private limited companies need not appoint a company secretary but if they do this must be notified to Companies House. Finally, plcs can raise money for the business through selling shares to the public.

A coach who sets up their business as a limited liability company and serves as a director of that company will not be self-employed. Directors and other staff become employees of the company and are taxed under the PAYE system and pay national insurance contributions accordingly. Apart from paying tax on your individual earnings, the company itself my be liable for corporation tax should it make a profit.

Advantages of a limited liability company

Despite the slightly more complex legal arrangements and duties placed upon the director of a limited liability company there are advantages in adopting this as the model for your business. It is a very good model for those of you who intend to employ other coaches in order to grow a business with a turnover that far exceeds what you could generate from working alone. It is not just your protection from full liability in case of business problems that makes this model appealing. The additional rigour which you must bring to running a business set up in this way can be appealing both to investors and to potential employees. It is also reassuring to families who might be resistant to your grand business plans if they fear it means losing the roof over their heads if things take a bad turn.

Setting up your business as a limited liability company implies seriousness of intent, commitment to good practice and transparency in financial matters. Of course many, many fly-by-night companies offer none of these things. Unscrupulous traders set up limited liability companies all the time with the explicit intent of evading liability for whatever dubious business they intend to conduct. You are not one of them. If you are planning a coaching empire or want to benefit from contracts, grants and funding that might be inaccessible to you as a less formally constituted business this is the way to go. Just be sure to get professional advice before deciding on this course of action.

CREATING A CO-OPERATIVE

Banish that image you have in your mind of a scruffy group of worthy, sandal-wearing bearded types endlessly debating which fair trade coffee to buy while disappointed clients find their calls go unanswered. Modern co-operatives are running highly successful business enterprises in fields as diverse as telecommunications, banking, grocery and bicycle sales. A co-operative can be run as:

- a partnership
- a company limited by guarantee
- an Industrial and Provident Society (IPS).

If you decide to run your business as a co-operative you will need to:

■ Decide on a set of rules for governing the way the organisation is run.

■ Decide on the ownership model and how profits will be distributed.

■ Decide what legal model you will choose to underpin the workings of your co-operative business.

■ Either notify Companies House (if you choose to set up as a company) or notify the Financial Services Authority (if you set up as an IPS).

Why choose the co-operative model?

There are local co-operative development agencies across the UK which can help and advise you on setting up your business as a co-operative. There is also a very positive and helpful organisation called Co-operatives UK (www.cooperatives-uk.coop) which offers excellent advice and information to anyone contemplating this option. Try www.cooponline.coop too. This is run by the UK's most famous Co-op – the organisation which runs a huge grocery sales business plus funeral homes, insurance and banking services among many more successful enterprises. Our high street co-ops demonstrate that a co-operative business model is a suitable base for business success but it doesn't explain why you might want to consider the model for your coaching business.

In the UK people talk of a co-operative movement and it is a subject that some people are passionate about. There is a recognised and internationally shared set of values which underpins co-operative working. If you look at them, and if you want your business to reflect these values, you begin to see why setting up your business as a co-operative might make sense for you. Coaching work must be underpinned by a clear set of ethics and values. Your business will thrive only if your clients trust you to meet your needs. The values which underpin the co-operative movement are pretty close to the types of ethical statements you might consider developing for your own coaching practice.

Values

Co-operatives are based on the values of self-help, self-responsibility, democracy, equality, equity and solidarity. In the tradition of their founders, co-operative members believe in the ethical values of honesty, openness, social responsibility and caring for others.

Principles

Co-operative principles are guidelines by which co-operatives put their values into practice. There are seven co-operative principles.

1 **Voluntary and open membership**: Co-operatives are voluntary organisations, open to all persons able to use their services and willing to accept the responsibilities of membership, without gender, social, racial, political or religious discrimination.

2. **Democratic member control**: Co-operatives are democratic organisations controlled by their members, who actively participate in setting their policies and making decisions. Men and women serving as elected representatives are accountable to the membership. In primary co-operatives members have equal voting rights (one member, one vote)

and co-operatives at other levels are also organised in a democratic manner.

3. **Member economic participation**: Members contribute equitably to, and democratically control, the capital of their co-operative. At least part of that capital is usually the common property of the co-operative. Members usually receive limited compensation, if any, on capital subscribed as a condition of membership. Members allocate surpluses for any or all of the following purposes: developing their co-operative, possibly setting up reserves, part of which at least would be indivisible; benefiting members in proportion to their transactions with the co-operative and supporting other activities approved by the membership.

> **Are co-ops old-fashioned?**
>
> *If you think the fastest growing consumer co-operative in the UK sells groceries, think again. This impressive achievement is claimed by The Phone Co-Op (www.phonecoop.coop), an unusual values driven telecoms provider which, according to Chief Executive Vivian Woodell, exists 'to help change things for the better rather than just for making money'.*
>
> *The Phone Co-Op provides all the usual residential and business telecoms services including line rental and broadband along with the feel-good factor generated by a business that puts people first. It is the eight-year-old brain child of social entrepreneur Woodell who spotted the opportunity offered by deregulation to apply the democratic principles of the co-operative movement to the telecoms industry.*
>
> *From a mess of paperwork and a skeleton staff housed in a spare bedroom in Woodell's Oxfordshire home back in 1998, The Phone Co-Op has grown to employ over 40 people, based mainly in Chipping Norton, and generates a £5 million turnover.*

4. **Autonomy and independence**: Co-operatives are autonomous, self-help organisations controlled by their members. If they enter into agreements with other organisations, including governments, or raise capital from external sources, they do so

on terms that ensure democratic control by their members and maintain their co-operative autonomy.

5 **Education, training and information**: Co-operatives provide education and training for their members, elected representatives, managers and employees so they can contribute effectively to the development of their co-operatives. They inform the general public – particularly young people and opinion leaders – about the nature and benefits of co-operation.

6 **Co-operation among co-operatives**: Co-operatives serve their members most effectively and strengthen the Co-operative Movement by working together through local, national, regional and international structures.

7 **Concern for community**: Co-operatives work for the sustainable development of their communities through policies approved by their members.

(www.cooponline.coop/about_whatis_values.html; accessed: 14 April 2008)

Social enterprises and not-for-profit businesses

Like a co-operative, a social enterprise can be set up as one of several different business structures. Indeed some social enterprises are also co-operatives and have been set up as Industrial and Provident Societies. Others are limited liability companies and there may well be some partnerships operating as social enterprises.

A social enterprise is really defined more by its purpose than its structure. A social enterprise is a business which has a primarily social purpose. It is normal for any profits to be reinvested in the business or the local community. It is unusual for social enterprises to generate a profit which is offered to shareholders or any individuals and this is why some social enterprises describe themselves as 'not-for-profit' organisations. However, you can see that it would be possible for a not-for-profit organisation not to fit the category of 'social enterprise'. Any business can aim to run on a zero budget basis (i.e. no profits are extracted from the business and any made are reinvested in the business and its people), but it does not need to have a clearly defined social purpose in order to be run in this way.

Social enterprise and coaching

Defining your coaching practice as a social enterprise might make sense if you are trying to coach in areas of obvious social benefit. This could include:

- Coaching people not in employment education or training.
- Coaching people from economically deprived areas who are suffering from lack of confidence.
- Coaching young offenders.
- Coaching people who suffer from discrimination.
- Coaching people with health problems.

Defining your business as a social enterprise would be particularly appropriate if you were seeking funding to make such coaching possible. Your status as a social enterprise would be appealing to public bodies charged with improving public health, employment levels and well-being. By clearly committing to reinvest profits in the business or the community you are signalling that any public funding coming your way will not be pocketed by sleeping partners or extracted to fund your new home in some far-flung tax haven.

Did you know?

A 2006 survey in Northern Ireland revealed that the upper quartile salary of a chief executive in the voluntary and community sector was £43,923 compared to £80,000 in the private sector.

(www.ukworkforcehub.org.uk)

Does this mean that it is sackcloth and ashes for the coach who models their business along social enterprise lines? Not a bit of it. If you develop an effective business and want to employ competent people you will have to pay fair salaries. Good business managers are often hard to find and funders, investors and clients will expect those who bear the brunt of keeping the business going to be paid a good salary. Even so, if you want to set up a business with the explicit intent of attracting funding from public bodies, from charities and trusts and other donors, your social purpose will have to be clearly explained and backed with a genuine intent to improve people's lives. Your salary should meet your funders expectations. Funding organisations take a dim view of tiny two- or three-person outfits claiming that the chief executive must be paid in the high five-figure salary band. Your salary in such a set up should be commensurate with your responsibilities and in line with public and voluntary sector pay. Take a look at the public appointments pages in the *Guardian* newspaper every week for a guide or log on to a website such as www.ukworkforcehub.co.uk for a clue to the going rate for a chief executive. The Community Accountancy Self Help group also publishes advice on financial matters, including salary scales, for charities and small voluntary sector organisations at www.cash-online.org.uk.

Could I start a charity?

Yes, you could. Some organisations that are registered as charities include coaching in their activities. There are very strict rules which govern how charities can be set up and run. Registration of charities is overseen by the Charity Commission in England and Wales, by the Office of the Scottish Charity Regulator in Scotland and by the Department for Social Development in Northern Ireland.

There are a range of fairly new rules governing both the purpose and governance of charities. One of the most important tests to apply to your proposal to register a charity is the public benefit test. Your organisation's aims must also fit with a defined list of charitable purposes. In England these include 'the advancement of citizenship or community development' and 'the advancement of health or the saving of lives'. It is easy to see how certain types of coaching, for example, coaching people for weight loss or smoking cessation, could be considered to advance health. It is possible to see how coaching which is designed to help boost confidence of people in communities with low rates of participation in processes, such as community planning, might meet the criteria around citizenship and community development.

If you want to know more about setting up a charity contact the relevant organisations. Full details are available as follows:

Charity Commission: www.charity-commission.gov.uk
Department for Social Development: www.dsdni.gov.uk
Office of the Scottish Charity Regulator: www.oscr.org.uk

WHAT IS A VOLUNTARY SECTOR ORGANISATION?

A voluntary sector organisation is typically one which utilises the work of volunteers (and often also paid staff) to meet its aims and objectives. This definition spans both a very small sports club which has no paid staff and works almost exclusively for the benefit of its members, and a vast multi-million pound income organisation such as Oxfam which works around the globe, employs thousands of people and deploys thousands of volunteers. The vast difference between two such organisations does suggest that the catch-all term 'voluntary sector' tells us very little about the actual nature of the organisations it is supposed to encompass.

The situation gets more complicated when you look at organisations which clearly operate for the public good but actually avoid using voluntary labour. Some so-called voluntary sector organisations are very uncomfortable about the idea of utilising unpaid labour. This is one reason why the term 'voluntary and community sector organisations' has started to creep into use where once 'voluntary sector' would have done.

My advice would be not to panic about definitions. If you have a business idea and a set of values that means you will be happiest running a business that appears to be more about achieving some sort of general social benefit than it is about feathering your own nest, then explore all the options open to you. You might find yourself at the helm of a thriving social enterprise, a brand new charity or a values-driven plc. As my dad always used to say, there is always more than one way to skin a cat. It is what your coaching training has taught you. Work out your goal then find a number of ways of achieving it.

CLEARING THE FINAL HURDLES

You want to run a coaching business? Figure out what kind of business you want to run, what level of risk you want to take on, what costs you are prepared to bear in setting up your business, on what basis you want to work with others and choose a business model to pursue. Although you could make an imperfect choice, you will be unlikely to make a seriously damaging choice that cannot be changed further down the line. All that you really need to focus on is that, as usual, a few minutes spent thinking and planning in advance of your decision will save hours of wasted time organising a change of direction later.

8

Marketing Your Business

Heard the one about the used-car salesman nobody trusted enough to buy a car from? You know that coaching relationships have to be based on mutual trust and respect. So too do coaching businesses. Unless you make sure your business comes across as one which can be trusted to provide an excellent coaching service you will not attract enough clients to keep your business going.

Who do they think you are?

If you had to choose a doctor to treat a damaged knee which of the following doctors would you choose?

■ *Doctor A: You see Dr A's advert handwritten in biro on a tattered index card. It is Sellotaped inside the newsagent's window sandwiched between ads for a second hand Renault Clio and a slimmer's club.*
■ *Doctor B: This doctor advertises in the local paper. The ad contains a quote from a satisfied patient described as Mrs X who is happy to have finally combated her eczema.*
■ *Doctor C: This doctor is recommended to you by a friend. Their knee works perfectly now that Doctor C has treated them.*

Which doctor would you be most likely to choose to sort out your own knee problems? Why?

Everyone attracts clients or customers for their products and services by using marketing techniques. At the market the fruit and veg seller traditionally used handwritten signs boasting 'cheap carrot's' and 'luvly apples' and belted out a few lines at top volume designed to make you notice the stall. The stallholder might even have benefited from being a longstanding trader with a family history in the business. Some indoor market stalls and older shops have bright, beautifully painted signs emphasising the history of the vendor with phrases such as 'A family business established in 1922'.

My granddad's butcher's shop in Rawtenstall, Lancashire, proudly bore the name 'J.J. Winterbottom & Sons' and I believe there were also signs to indicate that the business had won prizes for its black puddings. My granddad did this presumably because a family business, a business of longstanding which had been handed down through generations, would be seen as a business shoppers could trust. And winning prizes for your products is always a good way to signal quality. He wasn't deceiving the public. Some of my uncles did work in the shop for a while but in truth the business rose and fell in one generation. John James Winterbottom started it but my uncles eventually turned to other trades and my aunties did what women did in those days – got married and followed their husbands' fortunes. For all the Victorian, ornately curlicued letterheads, J.J.Winterbottom & Sons was a relatively

What is a brand?

This is a question that can be debated endlessly. Don't. There's no point discussing this while your business withers on the vine.

One simple definition of the brand is 'everything that your company is thought to represent or stand for'. The trick of good marketing is attracting customers by getting your company known and by getting your customers to think of your business in the way you want them to.

A business's brand is made up of everything that is said and done by any of the people associated with the business. You might call a cleaning company 'Kleen-Kwik' and advertise it as 'The cleanest, quickest cleaning service in town'. Will customers believe you if your staff work at half the speed of other cleaners and leave things dirtier than when they started?

If you remember that building a brand is about everything you say and do and not just your name and what you say in your advertising, you will be on the right track.

new business that lasted a relatively short time. It was, however, very successful in its day.

BUILDING TRUST

Businesses do not need a long history in order to inspire trust but it helps. People speak of 'household names' such as Marks and Spencer, Boots and Tesco. Marks and Spencer was established in 1884, Boots in 1849 and the Tesco brand first emerged in 1924. This is no longer obvious when you walk into one of their branches. Large retailers have moved on from relying on longevity and tradition to increase their popularity and their turnover. Perhaps there is evidence to suggest that the risk of being perceived as old-fashioned outweighs the benefits of being seen as trustworthy by dint of having been around for a long time?

Your business is new. There are advantages to this. People are excited by novelty. You cannot become a household name overnight. You are not in possession of a brand of which everyone has heard but you can easily avoid being perceived as old-fashioned. Well-established companies cannot any longer, if they ever could, rely on history as the basis for their marketing strategies. New businesses do not even have the choice. It clearly is possible to become highly successful and well-known without the benefit of a long business track record. Just think of Orange and Google (established in 1994 and 1998 respectively). They are very new companies, very successful companies and very well-known. But are they trusted? That's up to you to decide.

Sometimes businesses are successful but enjoy low levels of consumer trust. This can be because their products are so desirable that people are willing to overlook shoddy customer service, faulty goods and a myriad of other negative factors. This is not going to be true of your coaching service. Unless you are already someone who people would give their right arm to meet, you are going to have to market your business vigorously and build up a reputation for trustworthiness and effectiveness in order to attract sufficient clients to make your business viable.

WHAT IS MARKETING?

Marketing your business is letting people know what you can do for them. The trick lies in telling them in ways they want to hear. You have to capture the attention of your potential clients. You have to make them want to know about you.

You achieve this by:

- being clear about who you are marketing your business to
- finding out as much about these people as you can

What builds trust?

I took out a mobile phone contract with Orange. When I rang to set it up the call was answered very quickly. The phone I had seen online was available at the price I expected. It was sent to me within 48 hours. The instructions were easy to understand and my phone worked perfectly. My first monthly bill was exactly the amount Orange had told me it would be.

Later that year, I went on holiday in France. My next bill was four times what I expected. The dreaded roaming charges, which were not explained to me clearly at the start, had kicked in. Then the website stopped working well. I could not download or view my bills. When I tried the customer service number advertised on the website it was unobtainable. When I made an expensive call from my mobile I was told that the number had been taken out of service and that I had to email for advice instead. The man could not solve my problem there and then. Later that week, after emailing, a very friendly woman called me to sort out my problems.

I had high levels of trust in Orange when I first took out my contract, now I'm not so sure.

Can you spot which elements boosted and which undermined my trust in Orange?

- working out how to reach them and get their attention
- just doing it.

WHAT IS A MARKETING STRATEGY?

Your marketing strategy is the who, the what and the how:

- Who are you going to attract to your business?
- What are you going to offer them?
- How are you going to get their attention/reach them?

30-second marketing plan

You want to coach young mums seeking to return to work.

State three things you might offer which would appeal to these people:

1 ....

2 ....

3 ....

If they were not actively looking for a coach, state three ways in which they might find out about your coaching offer:

1 ....

2 ....

3 ....

See examples on page 130.

We have already looked at the value of targeting a client group which you really want to coach. This keeps up your motivation and helps you through the hard work involved in building up your business. If you focus on one main and possibly one secondary client market your marketing strategy need not be complicated. The more clearly you define your target market the easier it becomes to choose exactly what you will offer them and how you will get their attention.

In the example above, the target market is defined as 'young mums'. This is going to mean different things to different people. I was happy enough to hear a woman of 45 described as 'young' the other day but I doubt that same woman would ever be referred to as a 'young mum' no matter how recently she's had a baby. The life experience, interests and daily life of a 16-year-old single mum and school dropout with a six-month-old baby will probably be very different from those of a 32-year-old happily married, qualified lawyer with a five-year-old starting school. Both could be said to be young mums but in terms of whom you are marketing your service to and how you will do it, the differences between them will probably be quite significant.

- Are they both likely to hang out at mother and toddler clubs or to be found at the school gates?

- Do they read the same magazines, watch the same television programmes and shop in the same clothes shops?

- Do they use the Internet in the same way or might one be more into social networking sites than the other?

- Might one be more able to afford coaching than the other and therefore less concerned with affordability?

- Might one find it harder to get childcare so they can focus on coaching?

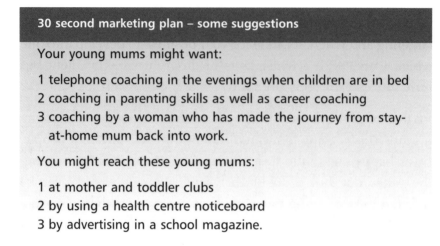

30 second marketing plan – some suggestions

Your young mums might want:

1 telephone coaching in the evenings when children are in bed
2 coaching in parenting skills as well as career coaching
3 coaching by a woman who has made the journey from stay-at-home mum back into work.

You might reach these young mums:

1 at mother and toddler clubs
2 by using a health centre noticeboard
3 by advertising in a school magazine.

You need to really research and think about your target market before you can create an effective marketing strategy. You cannot reach prospective clients if you do not know how to attract their attention. Even if you had a huge marketing budget you wouldn't advertise in a lad's magazine such as *Nuts* and *Loaded* to reach a client base of elderly, church-going ladies. The differences between different kinds of 'young mums' is obviously more subtle but important nonetheless.

HOW TO WRITE A MARKETING STRATEGY AND PLAN

This document should cover:

- who you are targeting
- what you are offering them
- how you will reach them
- when you will do this
- how much it will cost.

Your overall business plan will cover some of this, for example, your target clients. The marketing strategy should be the place where you really knuckle down and define exactly who you are targeting and when. It is fine for your business to develop into one which works with a wide range of different types of client but your success is more assured if you take this one step at a time. So, while your overall business plan is perfectly acceptable, if it identifies a very wide target client group or a large number of different client groups, your marketing strategy should be very focused on each individual group.

You cannot talk to all the people all the time. Your marketing strategy should show how and when you will try to reach which clients. As a rough rule of thumb try making sure that at least 60 per cent of your marketing effort goes into one clearly defined target client group before turning your attention to another. There is good evidence that a focused drive to reach and recruit clients is more successful than a scattergun approach.

Who are you targeting?

Try to be as specific as possible in defining your targets. For example, mothers with school-aged children seeking to return to work. This is more specific than 'young mums' and more helpful than an age group definition. Their interests will be affected by issues such as social class, education and age to some extent. It is helpful to cluster people into identifiable groups but this is not saying that they are all the same. All you can assume is that 'mothers with school-age children seeking to return to work' are likely to share certain desires, concerns, behaviours and attitudes. It is these likely similarities that will help you reach them. What might these be?

■ They share a common interest, i.e. getting back into employment.

■ They are probably in reasonably close contact with their children's schools which provides a route of contact for you.

■ They are all probably feeling under-confident to some degree, having spent time out of work and this could help you shape your marketing messages.

■ They may all be looking to update their skills. Certain organisations such as local colleges might be places to focus on for getting your services known about.

Compare this with another quite specific target group – for example, retired people in and around Chelmsford seeking to get more out of their retirement. If you were researching this target group how would you go about it? Here are some suggestions.

■ You could look at census data to determine the size and the potential size of your market.

■ You could look for any other research that described the hobbies and behaviours of such people.

■ You could contact local employers to find out if they offer advice packs or other targeted services to people approaching retirement.

■ You could contact organisations which offer advice, support, social or volunteering opportunities to retired people to see if they have any research data they are willing to share.

If you are starting a small, modestly resourced business your marketing strategy will always be based, to some extent on your assumptions about your target clients and their needs, behaviours, likes and dislikes. You simply will not have enough time or money to commission tailored research in order to find out what you need to know. This is not an excuse for not doing as much fact finding as you can. The more accurately you capture the scope and nature of your target group, the more materials you will have to work with when it comes to deciding what you will offer them.

What you will offer your clients

You must offer a coaching service that meets the needs of your target clients. This is not just a matter of describing your service in a way which makes it sound as if it will meet their needs, you have to adjust what you will actually offer so that it really does meet your clients' needs and, ideally, does so more successfully than your competitors. This means that your client offer should be continually reviewed. People and markets are constantly changing – sometimes slowly, for example, in what people are looking for in a home. Forty years ago house hunters would not expect an en suite bathroom in a family home or even think they needed one. Today's house hunters are very different. Speedier changes would include the mobile phone market. Five years ago few of us believed we needed a phone which is also a camera but now this is standard kit. Phones without cameras apparently do not meet our needs.

What if your basic product is not high tech? What if your basic product cannot change much and cannot be differentiated in any meaningful way from that being sold by your competitors? Take fuel for cars. All petrol and diesel is much the same once your car is bowling along in the fast lane but different petrol suppliers are out there seeking your business. One brand of petrol used to be marketed with the promise that it would 'put a tiger in your tank'. Petrol suppliers and garages have tried offering you a variety of freebies and benefits once you have bought a certain amount of fuel. Today you can notch up Nectar points. Once it was free key rings, storage jars and Green Shield stamps. Concern about the environment has led to fuel being described as 'cleaner'. Some garages go for the simple marketing offer – the cheapest fuel in Dewsbury; the last fuel before the M5.

Each of these messages describes what the garage is offering. The first message appeals to the price conscious, the second only to those about to drive on to the M5. Your coaching service is a somewhat more complicated product to sell then petrol or diesel but the principle remains the same. You have to decide:

- what you are offering
- who you are offering it to
- how you will make this offer so that it appeals to your target audience because they perceive it to meet their needs.

Your offer can be quite varied. It might include:

- telephone coaching at a time that suits you
- evening sessions for busy professionals
- free introductory sessions
- five sessions for the price of three if you book in advance
- achievement guaranteed or your money back.

The point is to tailor the offer to the target clients.

Give two reasons why the phrase 'evening sessions for busy professionals' is unlikely to appeal directly to young stay-at-home mothers with school-aged children.

1 ....

2 ....

Answers:

1 They are not 'busy professionals' so the words do not address them.

2 Evenings can be their busiest family time with a meal to cook, homework to support, bath time and bedtime.

Make sure that you do describe your business and what you offer in ways which speak directly to your target clients. For example 'telephone coaching at a time that suits you' is far more inclusive of the young mums market. Better still, it doesn't exclude busy professionals. If they are your secondary market this could be the perfect offer for both types of target clients.

What about the other options mentioned earlier? These were:

- free introductory sessions
- five sessions for the price of three if you book in advance
- achievement guaranteed or your money back.

What is the purpose of making such offers? Well, for example, an offer of free sessions has several potential benefits:

- It will appeal to the under-confident who want a low risk way of finding out about coaching.
- It will appeal to the price-conscious clients.
- It will help build trust in all clients.

Similarly, a money-back guarantee will make it easier for people to trust you before they have a great deal of direct or reported information upon which to base their trust. Of course, you have to live up to your promise. Not just because you could be in trouble with advertising standards and consumer protection rules if you make offers you do not intend to fulfil. You have to live up to the promise because that is how you build your fledgling business into a trusted name – a brand – a service which people are happy to be associated with and to recommend to others.

How you will reach your target market

Fife has the biggest obesity problem in Scotland and yet millions of pounds of public money were spent on Scotland's nationwide healthy-eating initiative as little as five years ago. This included a major television advertising and billboard campaign, work in schools and with healthcare staff. Most people in Fife must have seen the advertisements at least once. Even so, it is clear that a great number of people have not changed their behaviour significantly as a result. Why might that be?

This could be because the campaign was driven by the needs of the Scottish Government to tackle poor health in Scotland rather than the needs of the people of Fife. This example shows that, even if you could afford a major advertising campaign to promote your business, that money would be wasted if you did not make sure that the messages in your advertisements clearly showed how your coaching service will meet the needs of your target clients.

Your marketing strategy must be based upon:

1   Addressing the needs of your target clients.

2   Showing how you can address their needs more successfully than your competitors.

You then have to plan what mix of marketing techniques you will use to reach your target clients. These could include:

- advertising
- direct marketing
- media coverage
- networking
- word-of-mouth recommendations.

Advertising

The huge benefit of advertising is that you control the message. All the images and words used in an advertisement can be chosen by you. The major disadvantage is cost. Advertising in the print and broadcast media or on billboards is very expensive.

If you intend to advertise your business you have a range of opportunities which include:

- Local advertising (e.g. local newspapers, local radio, poster campaigns, posters and leaflets in local shops, health centres, etc.).

- Internet advertising (e.g. paid-for links on other websites, search engine pages, banner ads on websites).

- Advertising in the consumer press (e.g. women's magazines, Sunday supplements).

- Advertising in the trade and technical press (e.g. in publications targeting HR staff).

- Cinema and national radio advertising.

- Billboards (e.g. at bus stops, tube stations, large billboards alongside busy roads).

Even if you have ambitious business goals backed by a large advertising budget you should always ask if the vehicle for your advertising is fit for purpose. Take a look at the billboard ad campaigns in your area the next time you are out. How many advertise consumable products such as washing powders, clothing, beauty products, and how many offer services?

Now look at the classified advertisements at the back of glossy women's magazines such as *Red*, *Cosmopolitan* and *Good House-keeping*.

■ Which would you be more likely to look at if you were in search of a life coaching service?

■ Which would reach women most directly?

■ Where could you advertise to make sure your service was mainly promoted to men?

All publications, including websites, and all broadcast media that accept advertising will offer information designed to persuade prospective advertisers to buy ad space. They will tell you something about the size and nature of their audiences as well as the cost of advertising with them. They will often tell you about success stories – clients who claim that advertising with them proved to be well worth the money. Remember that ad sales teams are trying to achieve the same thing you are – they are trying to attract clients. Always:

■ Check claims about circulation/audience as carefully as you are able.

■ Speak to previous advertisers to assess their experience yourself.

■ Negotiate hard on price. Ad sales is a very tough market and large discounts on the first quoted price are the norm except for very small ads in the classified section of local papers.

■ Ask yourself 'Is this the most cost-effective way of reaching my clients?'

■ Ask yourself 'What impression will this advertisement, shown in this place, give of my business?'

The last question is vital. Although you can control the content of your advertising you cannot always control the context. For example, your highly professional service might appear less so if it were to be advertised on the same page as a feature about dodgy life coaches delivering shoddy advice at rip-off prices.

Finally, don't cut corners. An amateurish-looking photograph, a piece of written copy with mistakes in it or a poorly designed advertisement could undermine all that you are trying to say about your business. If you are planning to spend a significant amount of money on advertising your business:

■ seek professional advice on planning your ad campaign

■ get professional help in designing and writing your advertisements

Writing in plain English

Write in plain English if you want your marketing messages to be easy to understand. The rules for writing in this way are simple:

1 *Keep your sentences short.*
2 *Use active verbs where possible.*
3 *Use 'you' and 'we'.*
4 *Choose words appropriate for the reader.*
5 *Don't be afraid to give instructions.*
6 *Avoid nominalisations.*
7 *Use positive language.*
8 *Use lists where appropriate.*

You can find out more about improving your writing at www.plainenglish.co.uk. This is the website of the Plain English Campaign.

▪ work out how to monitor and evaluate the campaign.

The last is crucial. You have to learn from your experience to help move your marketing strategy onwards. You need to know, as far as possible, whether the advertising you pay for makes a positive difference to your business. Monitoring and evaluation need not be complicated. If you ask every new client how they heard about your life-coaching service you will soon find out if advertising is driving clients to you or whether they are coming having heard about your service in other ways.

Direct marketing

This is a tool you can use to attract new clients and to reach existing or previous clients. This marketing technique is called 'direct' because it involves sending a marketing message directly to a person. This is done in several ways:

▪ by mailing a letter or leaflet to your target clients
▪ by phoning (telemarketing), texting or faxing your target clients
▪ by emailing your target clients.

Most of us have been cold-called at home by people selling conservatories, double glazing or new kitchens. Cold-calling or cold-mailing is when a potential client has not previously expressed an interest in your product or service. They may be targeted because they fit the profile of a potential client (i.e. I am a homeowner so I might want a conservatory).

You can also receive calls or mailing which result from you having expressed an interest. This makes you a warm contact. You might, for example, have ticked a box on a form saying you want to know more about double glazing. Warm contacts are seen as better prospects for converting into potential customers than cold contacts.

You can check out average response rates to direct mail campaigns by going to the Royal Mail's website at *www.royal-mail.com*. A 2004 survey showed rates as high as 30 per cent with an average consumer response rate of 11.6 per cent.

There are rules governing direct marketing. You must be particularly careful when using electronic communications and you must observe rules around data protection in all cases when you are gathering and storing names of people. Full details of all the rules are available from the Information Commissioners Office at www.ico.gov.uk.

The Direct Marketing Association is the trade association representing the direct marketing industry and is an excellent source of advice and information about training and contacts. You can find out more at www.dma.org.uk.

Some businesses only directly market to lapsed customers in an effort to get them to invest in their products and services again. Coaching organisations have become very good at this. Some coaches issue regular newsletters or e-bulletins with news and information which are designed to encourage customers back to the business. Others invest in or access lists of names and send direct marketing materials with the explicit intention of attracting new customers. The most freely available lists are:

- the electoral register
- the phone book.

These do not tell you anything about the people you intend to mail apart from where they live. If you want to access lists compiled by others that are broken down into categories such as age, gender, income or interests, you will usually have to pay for them. The Direct Marketing Association offers a 'list search' function that enables you to find out about a huge number of lists which you can access (www.dma.org.uk).

If you do not intend to invest in professional advice in designing and writing your direct mail materials then do at least show them to someone else before you spend a lot of money on print and postage. You would be amazed by how often a letter or leaflet that makes sense and looks good to you is misunderstood, disliked by or fails to impress your target clients. The quality of your materials is as important in direct marketing as it is in advertising. If you are promoting a high quality, professional coaching service, a cheap, poorly produced set of materials containing mistakes will under-mine your image and perhaps lose you business rather than gaining it.

Media coverage

From the prestigious Radio 4 show *Start the Week* to the morning shows on local radio and the pages of national and local newspapers, editors all share a similar challenge. They have to fill the space. They have airtime and pages to fill with interesting people and features that will capture the attention of their target audiences. You can use this to your advantage. You can promote your business via the national and local media and it will cost you little more than your time and your travel expenses. Cost is not the only advantage. Hearing or reading about your coaching service in the editorial content of a media outlet, rather than just through advertising, helps to build trust. We are sceptical about claims made in advertising but if we see or hear the face/voice behind the actual business and we take a liking to that person then we are likely to trust them. This is true especially if a trusted presenter appears to be interested in and to value the ideas and services described by their guest. Trust can rub off on media guests.

How do you get your coaching service featured in the media? Follow this guide for guaranteed success:

■ Start with local newspapers and radio. They have low budgets and cannot do much to search out stories. They are interested in anything new that is happening which has local connections. You are local, your business is new. They will give you space if you approach them in the right way.

■ Find out which programmes accept guests/which parts of a magazine or newspaper might run a story about you and who is responsible for choosing the guests or the topics to be covered. A phone call to a local radio station asking 'Who produces the Fred Bloggs show?' or to the newspaper asking 'Who edits the women's pages?' will get you the names you need.

■ Make sure you watch/read/listen to the target media outlet. You want to be featured in a context that is right for your business and you want to impress the media gatekeepers by offering them an idea that is right for their product.

■ Think of a topical angle to help promote your business. If you are offering coaching in parenting skills always contact the media if there has been a big story on a relevant theme such as hooliganism or obesity in childhood. Some media outlets are forbidden from directly promoting businesses and only local media will cover a business simply because it is new. You have to show why your business or your service is interesting and relevant.

- Send a press release by post or by email to the right person at the right time. There is a model press release at the end of this chapter. Your headline and first paragraph should clearly signal topicality and the who, what, where and when details that are essential. Always include contact details and make sure any phone numbers given are lines which will be answered quickly. Use mobile numbers rather than office numbers if you are unlikely to be in your office to respond. Timing is crucial. Check out media deadlines such as when the news pages are completed or when the Sunday colour supplement is planned (always much sooner than the actual news pages of a Sunday paper). Glossy women's magazines work months in advance so information about post-Christmas weight-loss coaching has to reach them long before New Year's Day. Check out their lead times at your planning stage.

- Follow up your press release with a polite phone call to your named contact. They are under no obligation to offer you time or space in their programme or publication. Do not act as if they owe you anything or as if you have any entitlement to media space. You do not. Persistence can pay off but not if you become irritating or offend people.

- Make sure you are as interesting and your business sounds as interesting as your press release suggests you are/it is. Interviewees need to be sparkly, lively and engaging if they want to be asked back. Being knowledgeable is not enough.

The cardinal sin is being boring so make sure you give short, sharp, intelligent answers to questions in an engaging tone of voice. If you are interviewed on a very serious issue then making jokes and being bubbly might not be appropriate. However, displaying gravitas and good sense does not mean you have to lecture the audience or talk as if you were a miracle cure for insomnia.

Networking

Small businesses with small marketing budgets need to utilise these marketing techniques as fully as possible.

Successful networking simply means finding and making your service known among groups of relevant people. For example, if you want to gain contracts from HR managers you might choose to attend conferences targeting these people and make sure you hand out your business card to as many attendees as possible. A more sophisticated approach might involve seeing if you can get yourself invited to speak at the conference or perhaps give a presentation at some other event attended by your target clients.

If your market is middle-aged women in rural areas then your networking might be achieved by attending WI meetings and village fetes. There are networks of people everywhere. Some of these are completely informal – for example, the cluster of mums and dads at the school gates every day. Some are more formal – for example, a local arts forum which connects people with an interest in the artistic and cultural life of an area. Type the term 'networking organisations' into Google and a UK-only search will yield around 175,000 hits. Refine your search to find the types of networking organisations which might be of use to you and start thinking laterally. Where are the informal networks which might contain your target clients and how will you reach them?

Word of mouth recommendations

Word of mouth is also a vital marketing tool. Maximise the chances of potential clients hearing about the good things you can do for them by making sure all your clients receive excellent service. People who are happy with what you provided for them will tell their friends and family. Unhappy customers will tell even more people.

ARE WEBSITES USEFUL?

Most new businesses feel that they should be represented on the Internet. This is probably correct. Websites are very useful tools for allowing potential clients to find out more about you and your business. They are an extremely low cost way of showing what you offer, allowing people access to testimonials and creating a professional image for your coaching service. However, you must look very carefully at how people use the Internet before assuming that your website will serve as a primary marketing tool.

Websites will be stumbled upon by some potential clients seeking coaching services but with 704,000 hits for a UK web search for 'life coaching' you have to accept that the likelihood of most people ending up at your site via this route is slim.

Clients who have heard about your coaching offer from another source will go to your website in order to find out more. However, all organisations with a web presence need to work out how to attract visitors to their website. Websites do not, on their own, attract high numbers of potential clients.

You should look at your website as a secondary marketing tool. A well-designed website is an asset when it comes to communicating with potential clients but it needs to be backed by other marketing methods.

FINAL THOUGHTS

You have already been encouraged to think of your business plan as a living document which needs to be revisited to ensure you are still travelling in the right direction. Your marketing strategy needs to be regarded in this way too.

You must monitor and evaluate the outcomes from all of your marketing activities and revise your strategy in the light of your findings. It is not unreasonable to spend 20 per cent of your time on marketing your business. That's one full day in every five-day working week. You cannot afford to waste that precious time. Make all your marketing activities count by ensuring you know what is working and what is not working.

Example Press Release

For immediate release
21 April 2008

New coaching service tackles underachieving teens
Experienced local coach Prunella Powers has set up a new coaching service for teenagers which promises to improve exam results in just three coaching sessions.

'Teenagers can do better if they set targets and find the motivation to stick to them,' Says Prunella. 'I guarantee they will be able to boost results by at least one point above predicted grades after just three coaching sessions if they really want to improve. I am so convinced that I offer a money-back guarantee.'

Powers Coaching is responding to national research that says Britain's teens are being let down by poor schools. Pupils who fail to achieve minimum targets in GCSEs are less likely to find employment.

Local youngsters are already benefiting from the service. Successful client, Amrit Singh, 15, explains:

'I had no idea how to plan revision. My teachers always seemed too busy to take me through it and I was getting depressed about bad results. Prunella helped me focus on what I wanted to achieve and now I'm on track for As and Bs in the most important subjects.'

ENDS

For more information ring Prunella on 01234 567 8910 or email powerscoaching@xxxxxxxx.

Growing Your Business

You have probably realised by now that your business will only grow by increasing sales. You have to sell more coaching sessions to existing or to new clients or sell more new products and services if your business is to grow.

If you have pursued a successful marketing strategy your business will grow. It will not grow indefinitely as every market has its limits and external factors, such as an economic recession, which might slow or halt growth or even cause a downturn. No matter how good your service and how hard you work to realise an excellent marketing plan, growth is not an automatic outcome.

You can be caught out all too easily by changes in the rate of business growth. Invest too little in people resources and you can miss out on a boom and permanently damage your chances of success. Invest too much and bankruptcy looms if you cannot grow sufficiently to cover costs.

You have to plan your business growth. Planning for growth means working out in advance how you will cope with increasing demand for your services and how much risk you want to take on. The first major risk you are likely to take is discussed in the next section – the big move from part-time to full-time coaching.

MOVING FROM PART-TIME TO FULL-TIME COACHING

Many coaches start their coaching practice on a part-time basis. This can be an ideal way of developing a new income stream while maintaining other important responsibilities such as caring for children or other family members. It is also a low-risk way of testing your interest in, commitment to and ability to build a coaching business. Some new coaches work full-time in paid employment while starting to coach when their day job is over.

When you decide to start growing your coaching business the first choice facing you usually involves deciding when the time is right to switch from part- to full-time coaching. Sooner or later a part-time coach will have to consider whether a switch to full-time coaching is desirable or feasible. Ideally you will have planned this transition when you wrote your business plan. However, sometimes unforeseen events will bring this important decision to the fore. For example:

- You may find demand for your coaching becomes higher than you can meet on a part-time basis.

- You might be made redundant from your main job.

- You may find coaching to be so enjoyable that you find it hard to focus on other work and become frustrated by not being able to coach full-time.

What to think about when considering a switch from part to full-time coaching

- Is there enough potential business out there to justify this switch?

- If you are receiving income from another job you must plan for a temporary or permanent fall in income.

- If you are leaving employment to coach full-time and that employment gives you access to a pension or other financial benefits, such as life insurance,you must decide if and how you will replace these benefits.

- If the switch means a loss of social contact (i.e. you are no longer working most days with colleagues) you should explore ways of recreating similar social opportunities if you know this is important to you.

- Your new place of work, which is most likely to be a home office, must be made fit for full-time working. For example, your desk, PC and phone should be set up to help you avoid eye strain (caused by glare from windows) and other physical problems such as RSI-type injuries (caused by poorly set up workstations).

- Your coaching office costs will rise as you spend more time there. Heating, lighting and phone bills will rise.

- If you intend becoming more highly dependent on the stream of income generated by coaching you must revisit marketing plans to ensure you can maintain or boost the numbers of clients and the income you are receiving from clients to match the additional time you are giving to the business.

- If you are swapping domestic duties for more time focused on coaching who will take up the ropes? A switch from part- to full-time might affect more people than you. Impacts on others might be financial, emotional or practical – anticipate the effects and make sure you are ready to handle them.

■ Ensure you have stress-busting measures in place to protect your mental health and well-being. Starting a new business can be very stressful, leaving a job to go full-time in an existing business also ranks high on the stress factor scale.

You should have already registered as self-employed with HM Revenue and Customs when you started coaching part-time. However, if turning to full time coaching raises your anticipated self-employed earnings very significantly you might also have to consider registering for VAT. Value Added Tax (VAT) is a tax which applies to many goods and most services. Once your business reaches a certain level of turnover you are required to register for VAT. This means that every time you charge for your services you have to add a VAT charge. You must account carefully for VAT on all incoming and outgoing goods and services. The thresholds (i.e. the turnover levels) at which the requirement to register for VAT kick in, change from time to time. To make sure you are up to speed on the latest rulings go to HM Revenues and Customs website at www.hmrc.gov.uk. You can download all the appropriate application forms and find out the current thresholds at this website.

PARTNERSHIP WORKING

Information about setting up formal partnerships is provided in Chapter 7. If you want to grow your business you might look to forming a partnership with one or more coaches. This might be a suitable arrangement if you wish to capitalise on growing demand for your services but do not wish to move to full-time working at this stage. It is also a way of increasing coaching capacity without taking on the level of responsibility that becoming an employer entails.

Nevertheless, once you have formed a partnership you will have to negotiate more often on important business decisions. You have to factor in the extra time this will take.

Informal partnerships can work very well but are inadvisable as a secure means of growing your business. Coaching is a very personal business and clients are likely to be more loyal to their coach than to the business. Without a clear agreement between partners as to how clients will be handled – for example, who has the right to mail former clients to encourage them to re-invest in coaching – you can expect some stormy discussions at some point.

SUB-CONTRACTING

Sub-contracting means offering a contract to a third party that requires that they deliver the goods or services that you have agreed to provide to one or more of your clients. Because of the personal nature of the relationship between coach and client this is not a system in common use in life coaching. However, it is a perfectly appropriate option to consider if a corporate opportunity arises and you know you will not have the capacity to handle all the coaching personally.

Your primary consideration must be your client. Will they be happy to agree a contract with you that might wholly or partly be delivered by another coach? If yes, then there should be no barriers to sub-contracting out the work.

There are several more factors to consider:

■ Is sub-contracting the best means of growing your business or are you just nervous of becoming an employer?

- Will the sub-contractor maintain high standards similar to your own? Your reputation could be damaged by poor quality work.

- Will sub-contracting the work open up the risk of losing clients to a third party?

- Do you have the resources to design or obtain a suitable legally binding contract which clearly outlines the terms of engagement between you, the sub-contractor and the client?

Sub-contracting is not a way of evading responsibility for any aspect of the agreed contract between you and the client. Your client's contract is with you and you are responsible in law for ensuring the terms of that contract are met and for putting right any problems that arise. You cannot refer a client to a sub-contractor when problems arise. A client may agree to resolve problems in this way but this is very poor practice and you do not have the law on your side. This is why it is vital that your contract with your sub-contractor is drawn up by an expert.

This is easy to understand if you think about a contract for building work at your home. You agree a contract with the general builder Mr X for all the works. If Mr X brings in a glazier who puts the wrong frosted glass in all the windows who would you expect to arrange to put this right? If you thought you had to chase the glazier then wake up to your legal rights – your builder Mr X is the man responsible for sorting out the mistake. The law does not require you to speak to anyone else to get it sorted because your contract is with Mr X.

BECOMING AN EMPLOYER

Your business will break even if the costs of running it, including all the costs of employing people, are equal to the income you receive from clients.

Your business will be profitable if the income you receive from clients exceeds the costs of running it, including all the costs of employing people.

You might think it a little patronising to start this section with two such obvious facts but funny things happen to people's thought processes once they consider becoming employers. I would hope that you would want to become a good employer who provides excellent pay, benefits and conditions for your people. At worst I would expect you to respect the legal minimum terms for employing people. Either way you need to weigh up the risks and benefits of growing your business and becoming an employer. Once you become an employer you are responsible for the livelihoods of others not just your own. This is not a responsibility to be taken lightly.

Risks and benefits of becoming an employer	
Risks	**Benefits**
Financial commitments/overheads rise	Widens pool of talents/skills
Poor recruitments or poor management can lead to loss of quality	More people resources allows you to meet increased demand
More knowledge required to ensure compliance on health and safety, and employment law	Opportunity to work to your strengths and delegate weaker areas to others
Greater demands to communicate well	Shared workload
There will be more risks and benefits. Can you think of any?	

Recruitment

By the time you have decided that you definitely need to recruit a new person to your business you should be absolutely clear about what that person is required to do. This forms the basis of their job description. When you know what you need them to do it should be easy to work out what skills, experience, knowledge and levels of competence are required to do the job well.

All of this information should be written down clearly. This will help you run a fair and effective recruitment process. It will help reduce possible conflict further down the line if you are clear from the outset about important matters such as:

- the precise responsibilities and activities required of the post holder

- the hours of work and the main place of work

- other important terms and conditions such as sick pay, annual leave, working hours.

You may be required to register as an employer with HM Revenue and Customs. You will certainly be required to ascertain whether any recruit is eligible to work in the UK. All of the information is available from the HMRC website at www.hmrc.gov.uk.

You are not required to advertise posts. You are perfectly entitled to offer a job to anyone you want to offer it to. However, laws designed to prevent discrimination means that you must take care to show that you have not unfairly discriminated against anyone in your recruitment processes. All employers have a legal responsibility to ensure that no unlawful discrimination occurs in the recruitment and selection process on the grounds of sex, race, age, disability, religion or belief, or sexual orientation.

Interviewing candidates is a very imperfect way of assessing the fit between a person and a job. A skilled interviewer will do better than one who has no idea how to conduct an interview so you might want to seek out some recruitment and selection training.

Always take up references. People are reluctant to say negative things about previous employees as they fear being sued. It is still important to talk to previous employers and ask for a reference from a client too if your new employee was previously self-employed.

Contracts of employment

You have entered into a contract of employment as soon as you have made an offer of employment and it has been accepted unconditionally by the applicant. You do not have to provide your new recruit with a formal written contract but you are required to provide them with a written description of the main aspects of their employment within two months of the start of their employment with you. If you wrote this as part of the recruitment process then you are on the right track. Providing this written statement to all employees is not only a good way of minimising the potential for bad feelings, misunderstandings and conflicts, it is a legal minimum requirement.

The terms of a contract of employment can be oral, written or implied. In some cases the terms are stated in a job advertisement, emphasised orally at interview and then added to in a job description written after the post has been accepted. Should disputes arise either employer or employee might find themselves referring to several pieces of evidence to make their case. You can see why a formal written contract of employment which both parties agree and sign might be preferable. Sometimes employers place a clause in their contracts of employment which specifically states that the contract overrules previous statements or other written documents. You should always get professional advice when drafting a contract of employment.

You cannot change a contract of employment without obtaining the employees specific consent to the changes. If you achieve this then any changes must be notified to the employee in writing no later than a month after applying the changes.

Terms and conditions

You can employ a person as:

- a permanent employee
- on a fixed-term contract
- as a freelancer or consultant.

You can only employ people as freelancers or consultants if they are registered as self-employed.

Staff on fixed-term contracts have the same legal rights and you have the same responsibilities to them as you do to permanent employees for the duration of their contract. The advantage of a fixed-term contract is that it can end:

- after a specified period of time
- when an event has happened
- when a task or project is concluded.

Fixed-term contracts are useful for covering unusually busy periods such as when other staff are on holiday but demand for your service is high or for special projects. It is not good practice to repeatedly employ the same person on fixed-term contracts in a bid, for example, to avoid potential redundancy payments. The law offers some protection against this to employees. Someone who has been employed on a fixed-term contract for four or more years is classed in law as a permanent employee. There can be some exemptions from this but you would be wise to seek advice on this and reconsider your tactics. Trust is not easily built if your basic employment practices are unfair or dishonest.

Duties placed on employers

Employers are responsible for deducting tax and National Insurance payments from their employees' pay. You will need to develop a basic payroll system to ensure this is carried out properly and keep records of all the pay provided and deductions. HMRC provides a new employer's starter pack which outlines all the steps you have to take (www.hmrc.gov.uk).

You will be responsible for the health and safety of your employees. Most employers must have insurance which covers them against liability for injury or disease arising out of their employees' employment. Full details are available from the Health and Safety Executive at www.hse.gov.uk/pubns/hse40.pdf.

There are other rights, responsibilities and legal requirements affecting the relationship between employer and employee. These include:

- entitlement to maternity, paternity and adoption leave
- correct procedures for handling absence due to ill health
- the right to request flexible working
- the working time directive which governs maximum working hours
- rules around redundancy terms, notice and payments

- rules associated with equalities legislation, such as making reasonable adjustments for people with disabilities
- rules on employing young people
- rules governing dismissal procedures
- rules governing health and safety at work.

For more information on all of these matters take professional advice and/or access advice offered on government department websites and advisory services such as Business Link at www.businesslink.gov.uk.

Trade unions and the advice and conciliation service ACAS (www.acas.org.uk) are also good sources of information. The Health and Safety Executive (www.hse.gov.uk) and the Chartered Institute of Personnel and Development (www.cipd.co.uk) are also important sources of up-to-date information on employment matters.

Managing your people

Meeting minimum legal standards is only one part of the story. You will also have to work out how you will support your staff by providing:

- good quality management and appropriate levels of supervision

- clear policies and procedures covering a wide range of potential situations.

You cannot be a good people manager without becoming well-informed and investing in learning and developing as a manager. Part of your personal development plan should be the development of management skills.

Good policies and procedures can be borrowed and adapted from a number of sources. Public sector organisations often publish theirs and larger voluntary sector organisations often pride themselves on being very good employers. You can ask them for copies of policies and procedures to help you develop your own. Again, membership of the Chartered Institute of Personnel and Development will help you access good quality information in this area (www.cipd.co.uk). The workSMART website, run by the Trades Union Congress (TUC) is another excellent source of information on employment matters (www.worksmart.org.uk).

Take care that any adaptation you make to manuals on policies and procedures, and any which you draft on your own meet minimum legal standards and are fit for purpose.

SUCCESSFUL TENDERING

You have to accept that you may never find yourself having to grapple with the exciting complexities of becoming an employer unless you increase sales and turnover. You cannot afford to take on more staff unless you have the level of business that justifies the additional time and money costs of employing people.

If your business plan and marketing strategy keeps you focused on coaching private individuals you may never spot an opportunity to grow your business by tendering for contracts. Your sales will be to individuals rather than to organisations. If your plan is to target corporate clients or to enter a new market, such as the current drive to get people on benefits back into work, you may well find that you will be required to bid for large contracts by means of a competitive tendering process.

Tendering, which simply means bidding, for work often requires you to complete a lengthy, detailed process. For example, public sector organisations are bound by specific rules and have clear policies which govern tendering processes. They might ask you to provide:

- an overall cost for the work specified plus a budget broken down into elements such as salaries, materials, travel, etc.
- CVs of all the staff who will be involved in delivering the work
- copies of your equal opportunities and other relevant policies
- copies of your last annual accounts
- references from previous clients.

You can see from this that submitting a tender can involve a great deal of work. This means it is very important that you decide whether it is worth entering a tendering process. At minimum, the work you win should be of a value higher than the costs of submitting the tender. It sounds ridiculous but it is not always so. Time-consuming tendering processes that involved meetings as well as the time cost of the initial submission can end up costing you money if you are not careful. However, there are benefits to tendering beyond the obvious prize of occasionally securing a lucrative, large-scale, long-term contract. These include:

- raising your profile with an important potential new client
- accessing feedback on unsuccessful bids which will help you identify your strengths and weaknesses
- discussions during the process that can help you learn more about the needs of desirable clients.

How do I find out about opportunities to tender?

■ Keep an eye on national newspapers and trade publications relevant to coaching. Many opportunities are advertised.

■ Make sure you plug into relevant networks so you can make it known that you are interested in these opportunities.

■ Subscribe to on-line tendering information services such as www.publictender.co.uk which lets people know about opportunities in the Highlands and Islands of Scotland.

■ Talk to all your business contacts.

■ Look at the websites of likely targets. Public sector organisations usually describe their tendering processes somewhere and explain how you can make sure you see all the opportunities. For example, the Legal Services Commission carries this information at www.legalservices.gov.uk/aboutus/tenders.asp and the Department of Health publicises its tenders at www.dh.gov.uk/en/Procurementandproposals/Tenders/index.htm.

When you decide to submit a tender always make sure the document is of the highest possible quality. Get someone who understands your prospective clients' needs to read it through before you submit it. Correct any errors by getting the document proofread and always, always ask for feedback if you are unsuccessful. Good luck

10

The Ethical Coach –
Protecting Yourself and
Your Clients

There is no single governing body for coaching in the UK and no requirement that coaches be accredited, registered or belong to any professional body. There are, as we explored in Chapter 2, many competing organisations interested in supporting your work as a coach in return for a membership fee.

This chapter will draw on the standards being set by some of these organisations as well as guidance from elsewhere to define the key ethical issues that are relevant to your coaching work.

You should start by considering what being an ethical coach means to you. It is also well worth focusing on what high professional and ethical standards will mean in terms of business growth. I make no apology here for recommending you adopt the highest possible standards in running your coaching business. Too many coaches are cavalier in their approach to setting and maintaining standards. There is a danger of the coaching industry falling into disrepute. Don't let your business become the coaching equivalent of the dodgy car dealer.

This chapter will address the two sides of coaching ethics. These are:

1   The ways in which high standards protect clients.
2   The ways in which high standards protect you.

WHAT ARE THE RISKS OF NOT ABIDING BY CLEAR ETHICAL STANDARDS?

Would you buy a used car off a blatantly dodgy car dealer? Unethical practices undermine trust and trust is the foundation stone of a successful coaching business. Having clear standards, values and a well-communicated ethical code helps to build trust.

But there are other reasons for maintaining high ethical standards. You know that being a coach is not about being an expert advisor. Your challenge is to draw on the inner resources of your clients to help them achieve whatever it is that they set as their goals. However, even though you are in the business of continually reminding your clients that the power to make things happen resides in them, some of your clients will feel that you are a very special person. It is not unusual for clients to admire their coaches. Clients are often very grateful to their coach for helping them change their lives. Whenever someone feels grateful there is an imbalance of power. Whether or not a grateful client has paid you for the work you did with them, some clients will feel indebted to you. They may wind up feeling in awe of you, imagining that the power to make change happen came from you and not from within themselves. With this comes the risk of the client becoming dependent on you.

This is dangerous territory. There is a risk that you will begin to believe these myths about yourself. We are all susceptible to flattery. Our judgement can be impaired when our ego or our pride starts to dominate our behaviour. Both your ability to run a business effectively and the lives of real people can be harmed if you don't keep the impact and importance of your coaching skills in perspective.

It is very rewarding to know that your clients think of you as being an exceptionally talented person and that they may admire you for having helped them so much. You use positive feedback and praise to help motivate your clients and boost their confidence. It is wonderful to get some of this reflected back on you as their coach, but if the warm, fuzzy, powerful feeling you get from all this positive feedback is to be kept safely in check you need some basic principles to fall back on. You need a reminder of what a coach is and what s/he does, of what is appropriate and what is inappropriate behaviour in a coach. In short, you need a set of rules to help you become and remain an ethical coach.

> *The European Mentoring and Coaching Council requires its members to sign up to an ethical code. It will help resolve any problems arising from alleged breaches of the code. In serious cases when a formal complaint has been made it will take action against member coaches in accordance with its Complaints and Disciplinary Procedures.*
>
> *(www.emccouncil.org/fileadmin/ documents/ EMCC_Code_of_Ethics.pdf)*

WHAT ARE THE MOST IMPORTANT ETHICAL ISSUES?

This section will address six key areas which must be addressed when considering the ethics of coaching. These are:

1   confidentiality
2   equity

3   working with vulnerable groups
4   sexual relationships
5   terminating coaching
6   supervision.

Confidentiality

Number one on the list must be confidentiality. Coaching is a trust-based activity and without a promise of confidentiality there can be no real trust. You must promise that the identity of your clients and anything they tell you remain confidential except in certain circumstances.

This is vital to your ability to coach effectively. No client who believes that you might discuss what they tell you with other people will be completely honest with you. They may not even be aware that they are censoring themselves but you can be sure that they will.

What are reasonable exceptions for breaching confidentiality? These might include:

■   When a client reveals illegal or highly unethical activity.

■   When a client gives permission to disclose information to a third party.

■   When a coach needs to reveal details in order to benefit from supervision by a their own coach/mentor.

It is vital that these factors are signalled to a client before you start working with them. Some coaches explain these specific exceptions in a general agreement on confidentiality into their contracts which clients are required to sign.

When the client is not the coachee

The rules governing confidentiality must be particularly carefully defined when the client is not the coachee. This is often the case in corporate/executive coaching. Your fee and the contract might be agreed with an HR or line manager and this makes them the 'client'. Is the coachee, who is benefiting from coaching at her/his employer's expense, entitled to full confidentiality? What if the client wants a progress or outcome report to justify their expenditure? What elements of the coaching sessions must remain confidential and what content might be shared with the client?

There are no easy answers but there must be rules which you agree with client and coachee before you start coaching. Most good employers understand that effective coaching is based on openness and honesty. They also understand that the rules of engagement in the workplace often dissuade people from letting their true goals be widely known. For example, if your ultimate ambition is to get promoted just high enough and stay just long enough to gain the knowledge and skills required to set up a competing business of your own, you would be unlikely to share this goal with your current employer.

One effective way of assuring coachee confidentiality while allowing the client to monitor progress is to report on achievement not content. This could include:

- Reporting on attendance at sessions.
- Reporting on the number of goals set and achieved.
- Reporting on the number of issues addressed rather than the precise nature of those issues.

It is entirely possible for a coach to report on progress without revealing the content of sessions. However, there are grey areas here too. Should you report on your assessment of their levels of commitment, demonstrated, for example by their attitude to goal setting and achievement?

APECS, the Association for Professional Executive Coaching and Supervision, addresses this issue of coachee confidentiality directly. It takes a very clear line on protecting coachee confidentiality. It uses the term 'sponsor' to refer to the organisation or individual funding the coaching and 'client' to refer to the coachee. Its ethical guidelines are available to browse on its website (www.apecs.org). This is how APECS defines the issue of managing the boundaries between sponsor and client:

The coach or supervisor will:

- *maintain proper confidentiality of personal information gained within the coaching/supervision context;*

- *maintain confidentiality of the names and roles of those who are or have been coached or supervised;*

- *maintain commercial confidentiality regarding any aspects of the Sponsoring Organisation's business and plans;*

- *only disclose information from the coaching or supervision context to the Sponsor with the specific permission of the Client and then only if there are special reasons why this is in the best interests of the Client;*

- *be prepared to disclose to the Sponsor or the competent authorities any matter which indicates an illegal or illicit action by the Client or where there is a significant risk to another person or body should this not be disclosed. In such rare circumstances the Client should be given the first opportunity to disclose unless the timing indicates that urgent action is needed by the Coach/Supervisor.*

www.apecs.org/coachingEthicalGuidelines.asp#Setting

Equity

Two principle qualities required in an excellent coach is that they are non-judgemental and do not allow personal prejudices to negatively affect their client work. Being open-minded and fair in your dealings with clients is not just a foundation stone of coaching excellence; it is often a matter of legal requirement. For example, if you are or plan to become an employer or you are running a business providing goods and services, then it is essential that you are fully familiar with current and upcoming legislation relating to equality, fairness and discrimination at work.

Detailed advice on legal matters can quickly become out of date so this book contains only general advice. Government websites are a good starting point for the latest information, particularly the Department of Work and Pensions website at www.dwp.gov.uk which includes links to a number of informative sites.

Sometimes very small businesses and sole traders are exempt from aspects of employment law and rules designed to guard against discrimination, but not always. Even if you find that your business is excluded from any legal requirements to take certain measures designed to promote equality of opportunity or prevent discrimination, you have to consider how taking advantage of any exemptions fits with your role as a coach. For example, if you sign up to certain ethical codes, which underpin membership of professional membership/coach accreditation organisations, you may be committing yourself to definitions of best practice that actually exceed minimum legal requirements.

There is a lot to learn about if you want to be at the cutting edge of good practice. In the last few years there has been new legislation on religion and belief, disability and sexual orientation; the laws on race discrimination have been comprehensively amended and the legislation on sex discrimination was amended in 2005. On top of this, new regulations on age discrimination have come into force.

The areas where there is risk of discrimination which are covered by legal requirements on employers and often also on providers of goods and services are:

- religion and belief
- sexual orientation
- race and ethnicity
- disability
- sex and gender
- age.

Here is a brief guide to each key area of existing and impending legislation for England and Wales. Remember that laws vary between England and Wales, Scotland and Northern Ireland, plus case law is constantly evolving and thus changing the legal picture for those who provide goods and services. You must check relevant government publications and websites or trustworthy advisory organisations, such as the Citizens Advice Bureau, or membership organisations which specialise in employment law or general legal matters such as the Chartered Institute for Personnel and Development, if you want to keep on top of current and forthcoming legislation.

Religion and belief

New employment rules addressing the treatment of someone less favourably on a basis of their religion or beliefs came into force in 2003. This covers a wide range of religious beliefs, including for example druidism, but not political beliefs. For employers it can mean setting up suitable facilities for worship but the rules require no specific action in relation to the provision of goods and services.

Sexual orientation

From 1 December 2003, the Employment Equality (Sexual Orientation) Regulations 2003 (SI 2003/1661) made discrimination by employers and trade unions on the grounds of sexual orientation unlawful.

Discrimination in the provision of public services is not covered. The principles are virtually the same as for sex discrimination and sexual orientation is defined as having a sexual orientation towards:

- persons of the same sex
- persons of the opposite sex
- persons of the same sex and of the opposite sex.

Race and ethnicity

Most people think of race discrimination as being less favourable treatment on the grounds of colour or race. However, under the Race Discrimination Act 1976 in addition to colour and race, 'racial grounds' is defined to include nationality and ethnic or national origin. Part III of the Act also covers any 'goods, facilities or services' which are offered to the public or a section of the public. This means, for instance, the services and facilities offered by you as a coach. Direct or indirect discrimination by you will be unlawful.

Someone who believes they have been discriminated against on racial grounds by someone offering goods or services to the public must bring their action in the County Court within six months.

Any contract (for example, to buy goods or supply services) which includes a term which discriminates on racial grounds is void and can be amended by applying to the County Court to strike out that term formally.

Disability

Part III of the Disability Discrimination Act 1975 gives disabled people important rights of access to everyday services that others take for granted.

The duties under Part III came into force in three stages:

1   Treating a disabled person less favourably because they are disabled has been unlawful since December 1996.

2   Since October 1999, service providers have had to consider making reasonable adjustments to the way they deliver their services so that disabled people can use them.

3   The final stage of the duties, which means service providers may have to consider making permanent physical adjustments to their premises, came into force in 2004.

Under the DDA, mental health problems can be considered to be a form of disability and someone with mental health problems can use the DDA to challenge any discrimination they feel they have experienced.

Sex and gender

The Sex Discrimination Act (1976) covers discrimination against men and women. The Act has been amended to bring discrimination against transsexuals within its scope. Whilst there is no legal definition of transsexualism there is now a statutory definition of 'gender re-assignment' in the Sex Discrimination Act as amended.

Age

It has been unlawful to discriminate in employment matters on the grounds of age since 1 October 1996. The regulations do not apply to the provision of goods and services but they do apply to all employers, private and public sector, vocational training providers, trade unions, professional organisations, employer organisations and trustees and managers of occupational pension schemes. They cover employees of any age, and other workers, office holders, partners of firms and others. They cover recruitment, terms and conditions, promotions, transfers, dismissals and training.

In practice this means that recruitment can only be carried out with age restrictions in place when there is a legal or objective justification. For example, recruitment to the armed forces and police service can still exclude young people under a certain age. It means that there is no longer an upper age limit on unfair dismissal and redundancy rights. Your employer can only retire you under the age of 65 if they can show that having a lower retirement age for that role (not just for you) is appropriate and necessary. You also have a statutory right to request working beyond the compulsory retirement age which your employer must consider.

Working with vulnerable groups

Most people understand that children are more vulnerable to harm from others, both mental and physical, than most adults. However, there are also adults who are seen as 'vulnerable'. A non-offensive, non-discriminatory definition of a 'vulnerable adult' is extremely difficult to agree. There is general consensus around the idea that adults who might be considered to be vulnerable include:

- People suffering from or recovering from mental health problems.
- People with severe physical impairments.
- People with learning disabilities.

People seeking to work with children and vulnerable adults as volunteers or staff in organisations, such as schools, clubs, hospitals, colleges and a wide range of other types of employment, are required to undergo special checking procedures to ensure they do not have a criminal record or track record of inappropriate behaviour. You might hear this checking process referred to as 'obtaining disclosure' or 'police checking'. Whatever you call it, the process is simply one of an employer checking your identity by asking to see key documents to evidence your identity and current address and requiring you to complete a form. Your employer is then able to apply for any relevant facts about your background to be disclosed to them – in essence this is to check that you have no convictions or police cautions on your record that would imply that you are an unsuitable person to work with vulnerable people.

New rules in this area offer self-employed people an opportunity to obtain similar documentary evidence of their record. However, you are not required to undergo this process if your work is only with vulnerable people who have made an individual, private contract with you for coaching services. If you are employed to coach on behalf of an organisation, such as a college or a local authority, they will take you through this process if they deem it to be necessary. It will almost always be required if you are contracted by a third party to coach young people under 18.

For more information about the new rules and existing procedures go to:

www.disclosurescotland.co.uk – for Scotland
www.crb.gov.uk – for England and Wales.

More on mental health issues

When discussing potentially vulnerable clients it is really important to better understand the impact of mental health on vulnerability. Please do not assume that everyone with mental health problems, past or present, is especially vulnerable. Mental illness affects one in four of us at some point in our lives so you will almost certainly find yourself working with clients who have experienced or who will experience problems with their mental health. The most common problems (in no particular order) include:

■ depression
■ bi-polar disorder

- schizophrenia
- anxiety
- obsessions
- phobias
- addictions (including alcohol and drug addiction).

One of the most important things to remember about people who experience these illnesses is that they have not always been ill and may not always be ill in the future. However, the experience of being ill and the ways in which others sometimes react to mental illness can have terribly damaging effects on people's confidence and self-esteem. This suggests that there is often a strong case for including coaching techniques as part of the recovery process.

For example, the organisation SANE has some interesting self-help advice for those who suffer from depression. The following advice is taken from their website at www.sane.org.uk:

> *When the depression lifts, you will be your normal self again. Half of those who have a depressive illness never have another. Those who do have a second depression will probably not have a third; the number who develop recurrent depressions is very small. Continue the drug treatment conscientiously even after you are well again as directed by your doctor. Try to avoid the kind of stresses that may have brought on the depression in the first place. If you feel that the depression is returning, visit your GP or counsellor. [. . .] Above all, try to understand the nature of your depression and be positive about how a situation can be altered.*

This encouragement to be positive sounds like a classic coaching technique suggesting that coaching could play a valuable role in the recovery process.

But should you work with people who may have become very vulnerable as a result of their illness?

> Coaches must not attempt to diagnose or assess any mental health issue or specific problem where clients may put themselves or others at risk, but must act solely out of their personal experience, as coaches are not trained or licensed to make such diagnoses or assessments.'
>
> International Coaching Association, www.certifiedcoach.org

This must be an individual decision based on an initial assessment of the client and the coach's own skills and level of experience. However, as a rule of thumb it is not advisable to work with a client who acknowledges that they are or who you suspect is currently suffering from depression or another serious mental illness unless you can satisfy yourself that the client satisfies two key criteria:

1 They are sufficiently robust to cope with the demands of the coaching process.
2 They are receiving adequate treatment for their illness.

Use your initial discussion with a prospective client to assess the first criterion. You should always be honest with your clients and stress the hard work involved in being coached as well as the demanding nature of the coaching process on an emotional level. Remember that some forms of mental illness can lead people to temporarily lose touch with their true capacity for action. Just as depression leaves people feeling inadequate and often unable to act, the so-called 'manic phase' in another illness known as bi-polar disorder can cause people to massively over-estimate their abilities.

Unless you are an expert it can be very difficult to establish whether the feedback you are receiving is reliable or a result of illness. If you have any doubts at all about anybody's capacity to handle the coaching process you should always tactfully voice your concerns and suggest they think it over for a period. Offering a further conversation at a later stage reassures the client that you are serious in wanting to work with them when the time is right for them.

The second criterion is only worth exploring if the client seems very robust to you. Of course, the client is entitled to keep details of their treatment confidential. However, as a precautionary measure it is wise to ask those clients who say that they are under the care of their GP, a psychiatrist, counsellor or other specialist for a letter from the relevant professional stating that in their view coaching will be beneficial to the client. It can help if you provide the client with written details of what is involved in the coaching process that they can share with any professionals involved in helping them to recover.

> *Each coach must decide whether or not to enter into a coaching relationship with a client who is currently undergoing psychotherapy or other mental health treatment. Most important in making this decision is the client's welfare.*
>
> *International Coaching Association, www.certifiedcoach.org*

It is very inadvisable to work with any clients unless you are satisfied of their ability to cope with the process. When a suspected or actual mental illness complicates the picture you should always err on the side of caution.

This raises the spectre of prospective clients feeling that you are discriminating against them and unjustly denying them access to your coaching service. Be very careful not to let fear of being unjustly accused of discrimination affect your judgement. Although mental illness is not a complete barrier to benefiting from coaching, it is not helpful to anyone for an inexperienced coach to work with a vulnerable client.

Take the following steps to guard against disappointing or offending clients who fall into this category:

- Build up a list of contacts and organisations that can help and advise any prospective clients exploring coaching so that you can refer them for further advice if you are not prepared to work with them at this stage. This could include any counsellors or coaches that you believe to be better suited to meeting your client's needs. A referral should never be presented as a recommendation. You are simply redirecting your potential client towards what you believe might be a helpful contact.

- If you feel it would be worthwhile for your client to pursue coaching at a later stage then suggest a date for them to call you back for another discussion.

- Avoid making statements about the potential client's capacity or well-being. You are not the expert in their state of health, they are.

- Work out some of your own ground rules and stick to them. For example, I have chosen not to work with anyone who I know is already regularly seeing a counsellor or psychiatrist as in my experience it can be difficult for clients be clear about the role of the coach as distinguished from the role of a therapist. Your grounds for refusing a potential client should always be noted down in case of any follow-up. It is perfectly acceptable to say that you do not feel you have the right set of skills to help them at this time if this is what you honestly feel.

Sexual relationships

Don't ever consider entering into a sexual relationship with a current client. There is a very high risk that your actions could later be considered to be a form of harassment or abuse, no matter who makes the first move. Clients are vulnerable to feelings of dependency and unrealistic beliefs about the importance of their coach to their ongoing happiness. Like counselling, coaching carries with it the possibility of intense but inappropriate emotional attachments. Forming a sexual relationship with a client is an abuse of your power as a coach.

Terminating coaching

A client who is unhappy with the coaching experience is always free to terminate the process at any time, but what about the coach? Is it ethical to tell a client you will no longer work with them?

The answer is yes but the ethical coach will ensure that the client understands that this is a possibility right from the very start of their relationship. A clear client–coach agreement will help make this clear to the client at the earliest opportunity and should state the grounds for such a termination.

You should always consider ending a relationship when it becomes clear that the client is not willing to take any steps towards changing their situation. Indeed, to fail to do so could be seen as very unethical. How could you justify accepting payment for a service which you knew would not work?

Novice coaches are often very nervous of making the wrong

judgement call in this area. When things are not going well with a client it can be tempting to stick with it for too long, seeing a termination of the relationship as a failure on the part of the coach. It is true that challenging clients are an opportunity for developing your skills but it is always a mistake to believe that a client who refuses to do the work agreed at the outset is somehow your problem. You are there to coach and coaching requires action on the part of the client.

Supervision

Supervision is a recognised process in counselling and should be more widely deployed in coaching. Most counsellors who are accredited by a recognised professional body will have been required to undergo a minimum number of hours of counselling themselves before and during their training. Once they qualify, it is considered good practice for them to continue to work with a counsellor themselves in a process known as supervision.

In an organisation which deploys counsellors, either as volunteers or paid staff, this supervising counsellor will meet regularly with the counselling staff either in a group or a one-to-one format. A counsellor working on a self-employed basis will choose and pay for the services of their own supervising counsellor if they wish to or of they are required to do so under the terms of registration with a professional body.

The purpose of these meetings is to enable the counsellors to discuss challenging cases and to explore any difficulties they are having. Sometimes these difficulties are practical – the counsellor is looking for advice on how to proceed. Sometimes they are emotional – the counsellor might be aware of a problem and raise it with their supervisor. This can take the form of letting off steam and exploring their emotional responses to clients as well as appealing for advice. Occasionally though, the counsellor is not fully aware that their emotions are affecting the process and it is the supervising counsellor's role to help them recognise what is happening at an emotional level and move through the process in a way which benefits the client without harming the counsellor.

Coaches are not generally working with extremely vulnerable clients or those with recognised mental health problems, and so the risks of making mistakes which lead to damaging the client or themselves tend to be far lower than the risks associated with counselling. However, the potential benefits of working with a supervisor are just as great. There is great potential for learning through reflecting on coaching conversations and to do so in a safe, formal and confidential environment is of real benefit to any coach.

Unfortunately, we do not all take up this opportunity. In the absence of a standard registration process for all coaches there is no requirement for coaches to regularly meet with a supervising coach. Unless such a requirement is introduced it is up to you to choose how to proceed.

Benefits of regular meetings with a supervising coach

It is fair to say that the coaching process is usually less intense and emotionally draining or challenging than many counselling processes. Therefore, it is unlikely that weekly or monthly supervision, which is common in counselling, would ever be seen as vital in coaching. However there are other benefits of supervision for the hands-on practising coach. These include:

■ Keeping in touch with what it feels like to be coached which helps you maintain respect and empathy for and with your clients.

■ Having someone help you set and achieve your own goals which helps keep you focused on what matters to you. It is easy to forget your own goals and needs and start to drift when all your focus is on working with other people's lives.

■ Learning from your work with clients. Reflecting on the coaching process with a supervising coach helps increase the learning you derive from client work.

If you decide to coach full or part-time as an independent, self-employed coach without the back-up of a team or a manager, it is worthwhile seriously considering building a relationship with a coach you feel you trust and who can offer you a form of supervision. Even quarterly sessions will ensure that you benefit in the ways listed above. If you are anxious about investing in coaching for yourself before building up your client base and an income stream from coaching, then look for people in the same position as you. Use websites and message boards or networks you are building to find a coach who is also looking for similar support. Although the ideal supervising coach is one more experienced than you, you might find working for each other on a no-fee basis provides the most practical support package.

SETTING A COACHING CODE OF CONDUCT

Deciding on an ethical framework for your coaching practice is quite tricky. Working out how to communicate it to others is even harder. Fortunately, most membership organisations will require that members sign up to some sort of code of conduct so there are lots of examples out there to guide you.

Because membership of a recognised coach accreditation body is not a legal requirement, many coaches design their own code of conduct. This is unlikely to result in a sufficiently robust statement of ethical intent unless you have done a lot of research. It is for this reason that a model DIY code of conduct will not be offered here. If you wish to design your own ethical statement/code of conduct you should start by researching the various ethical and professional standards being espoused by organisations offering membership and accreditation to coaches. Some examples are given throughout this chapter.

The International Association of Coaching (www.certifiedcoach. org) requires that its members sign up to and abide by a set of ethical principles which are divided into three headings:

- *integrity*
- *professional responsibility*
- *respect for people's rights and dignity.*

Their Code of Ethics covers a wide range of activities relating to coaching. For example the rules preclude making false claims about depth and breadth of professional experience; they cover when the fee structure should be explained to clients, and require the coach to agree never to become sexually involved with a current client.

The requirement they make of members is clearly explained as follows:

> *Every coach who joins the IAC must pledge to abide by these Ethical Principles and Code of Ethics. This Pledge is recorded on our website and available to the public via a Member History record.*

CLIENT CODES OF CONDUCT

Many coaches also design a code of conduct for their clients to sign. This has several benefits. A client code of conduct helps:

- make it clear to clients what their coach expects of them
- signal that the process requires commitment from them
- provide a set of objective measures which can be referred to as

The European Coaching Institute (www.europeancoachinginstitute.org) offers coach training and accreditation to coaches who have graduated from recognised courses. Its statements about ethics and values are clearly signalled on its website.

The ECI identifies seven core values as the basis for professional standards. These are:
- *integrity*
- *honesty*
- *transparency*
- *excellence*
- *care*
- *professionalism*
- *accountability.*

grounds for terminating coaching work with a client.

Some coaches will include the details of this code of conduct in contracts which they ask their clients to sign. This is a good way of ensuring a client's attention is drawn to the most important requirements you will place on them. Clients who have difficulty acknowledging that lack of progress is linked to their own choices are likely to 'forget' that they were asked to commit to a set of rules for their coaching. It is very advantageous to be able to remind people that they signed an agreement with you and that the agreement placed behavioural requirements on them.

When you strike a very clear agreement with your clients before coaching begins you are framing the coaching experience for them. A good quality client–coach agreement will help your client get the most of the experience of being coached because it will:

- inform the client about what to expect from their coach
- inform the client about what the coach expects from them.

A clearly presented agreement will help establish trust in the coaching relationship by:

- managing client expectations
- setting boundaries

Client Code of Conduct

I agree to:

- Always attend all meetings on time.

- Always telephone at the agreed time.

- Always be prepared for the coaching call by:
  a) checking what I have achieved against my tasks
  b) listing what is still outstanding with my explanation for not completing the tasks and emailing this to my coach 24 hours prior to our next coaching session
  c) considering what actions may be necessary prior to sessions.

- Be honest about my achievements.

- Allow my coach to challenge me in order to help me make progress.

- Be willing and enthusiastic about trying new methods that my coach may suggest from time to time.

- Accept and willingly work on direct, honest feedback received.

- Work in partnership with my coach.

- Be prepared to work on all areas of my life with my coach.

- Arrange for payment to be made in advance of all coaching calls or meetings.

- Request any receipt required in advance.

- Send any forms back promptly and fully completed.

- Be prepared to step outside my comfort zone into an achievement zone with support from my coach.

■ clarifying standards.

Client–coach agreements can take the form of a contract or letter of agreement. Many coaches state the service they offer in a signed 'promise' document and ask that clients reciprocate by signing a similar 'promise' document (provided by the coach).

Whatever you call your agreement it is important that you include in it all the matters of most importance to you.

HANDLING RISK

Coaching is about helping people build the life they choose. While working through any process of change your clients will often make decisions that involve risks. They might choose to risk their financial security by setting up a new business, or to risk changing the delicate balance of family relationships by exploring new ways of organising roles and responsibilities at home. They might risk their personal safety by taking up a new adventurous sport, such as potholing or skydiving.

Are you responsible if things go wrong for your client?

The short answer is no, not if you steered clear of advising and stuck to motivating the client to find her/his own solutions. But in increasingly litigious times, many people seem to think that looking for someone to blame when life doesn't turn out as they wanted and aiming to acquire a fat compensation cheque is a perfectly reasonable way to proceed.

INSURANCE

Coaching does not put you at high risk of being sued. This is why many insurers and coach membership organisations offer low cost indemnity insurance to coaches. This type of insurance protects against claims that your work had a damaging impact on a client. This is generally only possible when the client can establish that advice was offered. For example, if a client could establish that you had advised them to invest all their savings in setting up a business that failed, they might try to sue you for compensation. As you don't advise clients this seems unlikely, but large coaching organisations that work with freelance coaches almost always insist that you cover yourself with this kind of insurance so it is worth seeking quotes so you know what kind of costs are involved.

If you do work with clients face to face in venues which are not covered or do not cover you with their own insurance you should also consider public liability insurance. This kind of cover addresses legal costs, including compensation, for accidental injuries. Accidents leading to injury are all too common. A friend of mine once slipped on a copy of the *Radio Times* she had left on the sitting room floor and ended up having major knee surgery. You place your livelihood at risk if you do not insure against claims for such eventualities. One carelessly discarded flipchart marker could mean the difference between prosperity and ruin if a litigious client steps on it and crashes to the floor.

Lots of venues cover you and your clients when you are working there. Some don't. Always check before accepting a contract to work face to face with clients as acquiring insurance for a short contract or one-off job might not be financially viable.

HEALTH AND SAFETY

Unless you work face to face with clients, the person at most risk of any health and safety problems is you.

Here are some tips for avoiding common problems:

■ If you work with clients on the phone get a headset. Sitting at odd angles with the phone tucked into your neck and writing notes hunched over a desk is a quick route to the osteopath. A wireless headset also lets you stretch your legs during calls.

■ Get a good quality desk chair and ensure your workstation can be adjusted to suit your height.

■ Ditch that second-hand filing cabinet with the buckled drawers. Back problems do not respond well to bending double over a jammed and overloaded drawer and pulling too hard.

■ Clear the decks. You don't think a few essential notes on the floor can do any harm? Remember my friend who slipped on a copy of the *Radio Times*? She has never played football since.

■ Being fully present for your clients takes energy. Practise relaxation techniques and learn to put your client's dilemmas away at the end of each session. Getting stressed out by other people's lives is not the way to become an effective coach.

HARASSMENT

Obviously you will not harass your clients but what if one of them forms an inappropriate attachment to you? Or what if you wind up being pursued by a dissatisfied client?

Such cases appear to be extremely rare so don't panic. However there are some simple steps you can take to ensure you reduce the risk of any inappropriate follow-up on the part of the client.

- If you coach on the phone from home use a line which does not carry your home phone number. Either rent a separate business line or choose the low-cost option of a separate number and different ring tones so your family or housemates know not to pick up your business calls.

- If you work from home, consider using a PO Box address or other mail delivery service that allows you to keep your home address to yourself. It must be stressed that I've never heard of a coach being stalked or harassed at home by a client but it is a theoretical possibility.

- If you coach face to face try to use a quiet but semi-public space. For example, many serviced offices have glass partitions so you are not alone in an entirely private space with a client. This limits the risk of any physical or sexual harassment taking place and helps protect against false allegations of such behaviour.

Again, it is important to remember that coaches rarely, if ever, seem to be affected by these problems so do not let this put you off working with clients. It is simply good practice to protect yourself and your client from any possible actual or alleged harassment.

MAINTAINING YOUR OWN MENTAL HEALTH

It is worth saying at this stage that there is absolutely no reason to worry that becoming involved in coaching will have a negative impact on your mental health. However, it is important to acknowledge that if you are feeling a bit low, distressed, depressed or mentally under par for any reason and you carry on coaching you are very unlikely to be supporting your client to the best of your normal ability. In fact, you are at risk of sending out a message that you need their support and that's not a good coaching technique.

Here are five tips for keeping in good mental health.

1 Develop emotional resilience

Good parenting helps you do this but we didn't all enjoy perfect parents. If you feel as if your moods peak and trough too wildly or that relatively minor events upset you disproportionately then you can do more to build up your resilience. It is all about stopping negative thoughts and replacing them with more positive statements (e.g. I am an excellent coach, I am helping this client, s/he will achieve the goals). The trick is to develop and maintain a positive attitude in which you look for good outcomes and refuse to let your mind linger on negative thoughts.

2 Build exercise into your weekly routines

A survey carried out by the charity Mind in 2001 found that two-thirds of people consulted said that exercise helped to relieve the symptoms of depression and more than half said it helped to reduce stress and anxiety. Six out of 10 of the respondents said that physical exercise helped to improve their motivation and 50 per cent said it boosted their self-esteem. Chemicals in the body, such as serotonin, dopamine, norepinephrine and endorphins, are known to have strong effects on mood and are released as a result of exercise. It is thought that this accounts for some of the beneficial effects of exercise. One plus point is that using exercise to help lift depression means that you start to feel the effects instantly.

3 Do something that you love

It is easy to spend your whole working week coaching others to follow their dreams and forget to make time for whatever makes you happy. Whether it is work, a hobby, a social activity or doing nothing at all, if you love doing it then make time for it. You might be the kind of person who is passionate about lots of things. If you want to know what activities should be top of your list then choose the ones which enable you to experience flow. This is the happy state of being totally absorbed in what you are doing to the point at which you lose all track of time. Creative writing does it for me and if I'm doing that before a coaching or other important appointment I need to set an alarm if I don't want to disappoint anyone by not being ready on time.

4 Find a safe place to debrief and let off steam

It could be your own coach who helps by providing supervision if you choose to find one or it could be your cat. Just don't choose a person who will get sick of hearing about whatever is on your mind.

5 Maintain a healthy level of social contact

This can't be defined. It is whatever is right for you. Coaching can be very isolating. You work with people but clients are not your friends and you cannot really relax with them. Studies show that having lots of friends and seeing them as often as feels right for you is an excellent protector against depression and problems with self-esteem. Treat social events like you do important business appointments. Put them in your diary and never cancel them if you can avoid it. Feeling too tired to go out is often a sign that an hour or two laughing and chatting with some friends is just what you need to unwind. Your friends, colleagues and family are your support network. Make sure yours is strong enough to cope when you actually need support.

There are a host of other sensible suggestions that you can add to this list, such as eating healthily, steering clear of excessive stimulants and damaging drugs such as excess alcohol, getting enough sleep and avoiding becoming the listening ear for all your most unhappy friends. The point is that if you work on the top five listed above you are likely to maintain the will and the ability to manage all the others without having to think about it too much.

11

Writing Your Business Plan

If you have worked through each chapter systematically you will by now have your ambitions for your coaching business clear in your mind. You should know what type of business you want to launch, what type of clients you will target, how you will target them and how to conduct yourself professionally and safely. What comes next?

You are a coach. You know what comes next. You understand that getting what you want out of life is made more achievable when you set some clear goals and take the actions required to achieve those goals. You would be amazed to find how many so-called coaches seem to forget this simple rule when they start out in business. It is truly frightening how many people leap into running a business without ever working out where they are going and how they will get there. You only have to watch one episode of the BBC's *Dragon's Den*, in which would-be entrepreneur's pitch to a panel of wealthy business people for start-up or development funding, to notice how few people lay firm foundations for their dreams in the form of a well-thought-out business plan.

It is possible to start a coaching business by investing little more than a few pounds in business cards and the hidden cost of your spare time. Maybe this is why coaches seem particularly prone to trying to build a business empire on little more than the back-of-a-fag-packet type calculation. But your business dreams can all too easily be shattered if you do not take the time to plan ahead. From the moment that you suspect that starting a coaching business might be the best way forward for you, you should be planning how to go about it. This chapter advocates a systematic approach to business planning which will help you:

- decide whether you really want to run a coaching business at all

- decide what type, size and scale of coaching business you will build

- work out how to make your business successful in the immediate, medium and long term.

WHAT A BUSINESS PLAN TELLS THE WORLD

A business plan should tell anyone who sees it that you are serious about and committed to developing a successful coaching business. It must:

- explain what type of coaching service will be provided and how it will be provided

- clearly state the target clients for your coaching service

- clearly show how you will reach these clients and attract them to your business

- clearly show that your have researched the competition

- clearly show that there is a market for your coaching services

What my business will get for me

Do you remember what you decided you wanted from building your dream coaching business after reading Chapter 3?

Keep those important 'wants' in focus when you write your business plan.

Write them here to help you stay focused on them.

What I want to get from running my own coaching practice is:

....

....

....

The time I want to spend on running my business is:

....

....

....

The amount of money I want to make from running my business is:

....

....

....

- show how the business will be set up

- indicate how the business will grow

- back up all your goals with basic financial facts and figures which show how much money your business will cost to run, the turnover and the anticipated profits.

Your business plan should be more than a list of data. It should express what you intend to do in your coaching work, what type of person you intend to coach and how you intend to make it happen. All of this should be achieved in short, easy to read sentences which create a positive, clear image of your intentions in the mind of any reader.

A business plan is a goal-setting exercise. It is an important document and you should strive to write one which is robust and which can be used like a road map to help you reach your destination. However, it should never be a straitjacket. We are not talking tablets of stone here. A business plan is not a casual piece of writing that should be endlessly tinkered with but it should be a living document. By this I mean you should be open to new ideas and when a better idea, a new opportunity or alternative comes along you might need to adjust your plan to allow for it.

Using your business plan to access funds/ grants/investment

Business plans are not just your own private road map showing your route to success. They are important tools for persuading others to support your new enterprise. For example, if you need to borrow money to fund your business start-up costs you will need to convince others that your business will provide a return on that investment. High street banks and other money-lending institutions will demand evidence that a new business is well planned and viable before they will agree any loans. They prefer to see business plans written and expressed in a standard style. There are lots of organisations offering advice on writing business plans. Some of them are also investors. Make sure you explore the advice on offer from any potential source of credit or investment before you write your plan. The advice given here will enable you to write a plan based on a standard format that will be acceptable to many organisations. If you have a particular organisation you want to impress with your business plan then make sure you also check out any advice they offer on writing a sound, informative and impressive business plan.

The other really important point about business plans is that the process of writing one requires that you research your ideas and proposals thoroughly. This boosts the chances of your success because:

- you will be more likely to spot potential pitfalls and therefore avoid them

- you will be well prepared when matters beyond your control raise challenges for you and your business.

Once you have mastered the standard requirements of a convincing business plan there is no reason why you should not add more elements. In fact, the basic business plan can turn out to be a very uninspiring document and that is the last thing you need to keep your own motivation levels high. Lots of entrepreneurs produce a variety of 'plans' which contain the same core elements but which are written to meet different purposes.

For example, your bank or building society manager will need to know that you have a clear target market and plans in place for marketing your services effectively. They need to be confident that you will secure the level of business required to become profitable but they will rarely be interested in the precise detail of who will do what and when you will do it. You will find it helpful to develop an additional marketing plan with far more detail so that you and anyone working with you is clear about what needs to be done, how much it will cost, what resources are required and who will do what and when.

Free advice on business planning

www.businesslink.gov.uk – offers a wide range of practical advice to new and existing businesses and a postcode search function to put you in touch with local sources of advice.

www.bgateway.com – linked to the above. The website provides advice on all aspects of starting a business as well as a library of sample business plans and a full guide to business planning.

www.natwest.com – offers free business planning software and downloadable advice to people starting businesses. Try other high street banks for similar products and advice.

www.hbv.org.uk – local authorities and small agencies such as the Hackney Business Venture are a good source of information for small businesses. Some organisations, such as this one in London's Hackney, run free courses on planning your business; others provide advice on start-up grants and other means of helping you get started. Your local authority's website will usually direct you to local relevant services.

MIXING THE INGREDIENTS OF YOUR BUSINESS PLAN

A well-written and clearly presented business plan will produce a positive reaction in potential investors and supporters. Remember that it isn't just potential financiers you need to impress. Your whole family will be affected by your decision to start a business. There are always risks involved and you want a support network around you, urging you on. You don't want to be surrounded by people who do not understand what you are trying to achieve. A plan which follows a logical step-by-step approach will also be easier for you to follow.

These are the key elements that every business plan should include:

- **An executive summary** – a short, motivating overview of the business you want to start. It is a summary of your whole plan and you will find it easiest to write this when you have completed your plan.

- **Who, what, why and who** – who you are, what you will offer, why the service is needed/will be in demand, and to whom you will offer it.

- **Marketing and sales strategy** – why people will buy your coaching services and how you will sell coaching services to people. This section must show:
  - who your competitors are, what they offer and how you will compete successfully with them
  - how you will attract clients to your coaching service.

- **Who will manage and deliver the coaching service** – this is about you and anybody you will employ or team up with to make the business work.

Are you ready to write your plan?

Before you write your plan make sure your personal goals are clear in your mind. Check if you have:

- *explored ideas around creating the ideal life for you*
- *thought about what type of coaching might be right for you (e.g. corporate, personal, voluntary)*
- *decided what you need in terms of income to create and sustain your ideal life*
- *considered potential target markets*
- *come up with your own unique selling proposition.*

- **The inner workings of your business** – this is the operational part of the plan. You must show where you will be based, and how information and administrative functions will work.

- **The money** – you must include financial forecasts. Everything that goes into setting up and running your business has to be shown in terms of costs. This is the place for your financial goals. It must show how much money will be invested in making the business work and how much money will be raised from your coaching business. Ideally your forecasts will show a difference between the two – a difference that eventually shows your profits rather than losses.

Make sure your business plan is a document which you actually enjoy reading and which you can take in quickly, almost at a glance. Remember, it is a living document and should be kept close at hand, not filed away under a heap of dusty paperwork.

A STEP-BY-STEP GUIDE TO WRITING THE PLAN

State your goals

Your plan should always include a clear set of business goals. These can be very simple and should back up and not undermine your personal goals.

Stick to the principles of coaching when you set your business goals. Make sure the goals you write down are:

- challenging
- written in a positive manner
- easy to understand
- relevant
- not contradictory.

Then make sure your goals are SMART:

- **S**pecific: e.g. the business will target young people (16–25) not in employment, education or training.

- **M**easurable: e.g. the business will attract at least 12 paying clients in the first three months.

- **A**greed: e.g. the business will work in partnership with the local council under the terms of the contract agreed on 18 October 2007.

- **R**ealistic: e.g. the business will receive £25,000 in fees for coaching services in year 1.

- **T**ime phased: e.g. the client base will grow to 80 paying clients by the end of the first year.

Who, what, why and who?

Who are you?

When people invest in your business they are investing in you. This is the place to emphasise your skills and qualities. You have to come across as both a competent coach and a competent businessperson. Make this section brief and impressive. You can attach your CV to a business plan to provide additional detail if you think it is important.

What is your business offering?

Offer a clear and concise description of your proposed coaching service. For example:

■ A mainly telephone-based life-coaching service.

■ A face-to-face corporate coaching service provided at the client's place of work for their convenience.

■ A web- and telephone-based 24-hour coaching service offering same-day appointments.

The mode of delivery of your coaching service is important so make sure you include sufficient detail so that everyone understands the precise nature of what your business will offer.

Why this business, why now?

You know what you hope to gain from starting this business. This is not a good enough reason for starting a business. You have to show that this business is needed and that your service will be in demand. You know your own, personal reasons for starting a business but the plan is where you have to show the external reasons for starting the specific business you are describing.

You can illustrate these things by showing that the level of demand (see the next section about your target customers) and the timing of the development of your business are right. Don't use jargon – stick to language anybody, friends or family, will understand.

If you cannot show that the external conditions are right for starting this business you should have a rethink.

Who are your intended customers?

This is the place to describe them and to show very clearly how your services will meet their needs. This can involve a fair bit of research. For example, if you have chosen to work with women returning to paid work after time spent at home with their children you might need to find out more about them. For example, you might want to find out:

- what needs they have that coaching could meet
- how many of these kind of people there are
- average income levels (can they afford your service?).

Only you can decide how much of your time and money you want to put in to researching the basis for your business plan. Every business stands a greater chance of success if the business plan is based on sound research. However, the financial investment you make in the research will add to your start-up costs and the time you spend on research will also prevent you from doing other things.

You must find a balance between risk and investment which meets your needs. As a rule of thumb, the more risks you are taking when starting a business, for example, re-mortgaging your house to fund the start-up or giving up a lucrative job to run the business full-time, the more important it is that you invest in sound research.

Market research

When researching any target market always ask yourself the following questions:

- What is the typical age group you are targeting?
- Where are they based?
- How many of them are there in the UK, in your region, in your town?
- What is their income level?
- When are they likely to be able to take part in coaching sessions (if you do not want to work in the evenings this information could be vital)?

Personal data such as this can be hard to come by. You are trying to build up a picture of your client base which will help you make a number of very important decisions. These include:

- the potential size of your market
- ways of reaching your potential clients and marketing your services effectively to them
- whether face-to-face working is viable
- your fee -charging structure.

Commissioning professional market research is possible but it is costly. Some organisations publish the kind of data you might find helpful and make it available free of charge via libraries and/or the Internet. Local authorities and educational establishments can be excellent sources of information. They are required to respond to the needs of local people and often conduct their own research to ensure they are keeping alert to emerging needs and changes in the demographics of the area.

Demographics
Demography is the study of people-related statistics, for example, births, deaths, diseases and other aspects of human life for the purpose of illustrating conditions of life in specific communities.

Demographic segmentation is a phrase used in marketing to describe the breaking down of the general population into groups of people who share similar characteristics.

One example of a form of demographic segmentation is life-stage segmentation. Women returners are a good example of a group of people who have reached a similar stage in life. They are not all the same age (although they are likely to be aged between 25 and 55) but what makes them similar are the changes in their family life. In this case, the life stages they are at could be further broken down into three distinct categories:

1 Women whose youngest child is about to start school.
2 Women whose youngest child is about to start secondary school.
3 Women whose youngest child is about to leave home.

This does not mean that women who do not fit into these groups might not benefit from your services, or indeed men. After all, there will be people who have been carers for elderly relatives who might also be in need of coaching as they contemplate starting or restarting their careers. As you come across exceptions you can add them to your research. You might be surprised at what you find. For example, while still tiny in comparison with the number of women, the number of men taking a career break to care for their children is on the increase. Keeping an eye on demographics helps you to spot trends and to plan accordingly.

DIY research vs professional research
When you cannot find what you think you need to know using free sources of information and you do not have the budget to commission research then you have two options:

1 Do your own research.
2 Study the achievements and tactics of other businesses which are reaching the same or similar target market.

Doing your own research directly with the potential clients, for example, by constructing a questionnaire and knocking on doors or standing in the street to find people prepared to answer your questions, can be very time consuming and results can be misleading if you are not familiar with some of the principles of market research. Carefully assessing the achievements of others and gathering information from other organisations is a more reliable and less time consuming substitute for professional market research data. For example, you could:

■ call local employment services and ask them about women returners and how many approach their service

■ contact your local college and, if it runs specific courses for women returners, ask them to tell you how much demand there is for their courses.

Taking this target group of women returners as our example you might also want to explore the following:

■ Are there a high number of well-attended mother and toddler groups in the area indicating a substantial pool of stay-at-home mothers?

■ Is demand for childcare on the increase suggesting a growing number of mothers in employment outside the home?

Looking at other organisations and businesses which are targeting the same group of people can help indicate the strength of your potential market. This is what is happening when three coffee bars open up in swift succession on the same stretch of the high street. Once one pioneer opens up and proves there is demand others swoop in either to pick up on unmet demand (for example, if the first coffee place is too full) or to offer something extra in order to attract customers away from the pioneers.

The most important thing to remember is that you should not construct your entire business plan around a preferred target market until you have some knowledge or evidence to support your belief that:

■ the group exists
■ there are enough people in it to keep your business going
■ they have the income necessary to pay your fees or there is an organisation likely to fund you to work with these people
■ there is a need that your service will meet.

Marketing and sales strategy

Once you are clear about your target market you can start planning how you will reach it in order to attract clients.

There are two elements you need to consider:

1 Your marketing strategy – who you are targeting, what you are offering, how many will you target and over what period of time.

2 Your marketing plan – how you will do it, who will do it, specific activities identified and timetabled, the budget required for this activity, how you will manage the response to your marketing and how you will monitor and review progress.

At this stage in the business planning process you only need to show your overall marketing strategy.

This is the moment when you might be relieved to know that business planning is never a linear process. If you have chosen a target market that is going to be particularly hard to reach you might only realise this when you start to focus on your marketing strategy. Don't panic. You have two main options:

1   Go back and explore broadening/narrowing or adjusting your target market so that it still fits with your overall goals but makes the marketing easier.

2   Stick with it at this stage and seek some expert input on the marketing side. You might be surprised to find how many people will help you for free. It might be that you are too inexperienced to know the best means of targeting these people and what looks like a fatal flaw might only be a temporary obstacle. Be prepared to change direction later if your original instincts are proved to be correct.

Competitor analysis

Who are your competitors? Who is offering a service which is the same or similar to yours? This is vital information if you want to ensure that your business is viable. Remember your unique selling proposition? This is the statement which differentiates you from your competitors. You need to know who your competitors are and what they offer before you can really generate the best USP for your business.

This is another area requiring some research. You need to understand as much as you can about your competitors. Sometimes you will find the information you need on their websites or in their marketing materials. Sometimes you will need to pose as a potential customer or track down actual customers to discover facts, such as the cost of the service and the actual quality of the service on offer.

Don't skimp on this piece of research. If you were opening a new cafe wouldn't you go to eat at the other local cafes first to see how busy they were, what was on the menu, how well it was cooked, how big the portions were, what it cost and whether there was anything special about the service which customers found attractive? Starting a coaching service is just the same. You need to know what other people are offering as part of their service and who they are offering it to.

Questions you should ask include:

- Who are your competitors?
- Is the service they offer the same as yours?
- Do they provide something you haven't been planning to provide?
- Are they targeting the same clients as you?
- Can you find out what share they have of this market?
- How do they market themselves and can you do it better?
- What levels of service do their customers expect and can you find a way of surpassing this?

Who will manage and deliver the coaching service?

If you are setting up in business as a sole trader this should be made clear. If you are working on your own to deliver a coaching service then all the information required under this heading will have been provided already under in the first 'who' part of 'Who, what, why and who?'. But what if you plan to build your business by harnessing the energy of others?

If you are pulling together a team of people then you must make it clear how this new business will be organised. Is it going to be run as:

- a partnership
- a co-operative
- a group of employees managed directly by you
- a group of employees managed by a senior management team?

The legal aspects of how your business will be set-up and run are important. The people and the ideas are even more so. This information is what will motivate others to support your business. If you have a strong, experienced management team in place, especially if the people involved have a track record of success, make sure you mention it here.

If you are planning to employ others then make sure you include an explanation of the pay and benefits system. For example, will your business:

- offer a flat rate of pay to all or starting pay linked to skills or experience
- offer pay increases or bonuses linked to productivity
- offer more than the minimum legal holiday entitlement
- contribute to employees' pensions
- invest in staff training?

You will also incur recruitment costs. These will be significant when you start up and must be budgeted for throughout the life of your business. This means that another useful piece of data to include is your anticipated turnover rate – i.e. how long people are likely to stay in their jobs working in your business. Average figures for certain industries can be high. Can you find out what it is in coaching?

Operational requirements

Your operational requirements are what you need to put your plans into action. The good news for you if you are intending to become a self-employed coach is that all a coach really needs in order to start work is a telephone, a pencil, paper and a quiet place to work.

This is the standard list of potential operational requirements you should address in your plan:

- premises
- equipment (including IT)
- management systems
- people
- suppliers
- regulation and licensing.

The last operational requirement is unlikely to be essential for a coach working as a sole trader but it can be vital to some businesses. For example, there are a large number of statutory requirements which apply to businesses involved in childcare. If you do choose to employ other coaches you will need to be clear about any statutory obligations which are placed on you as an employer.

As a coach it is not a statutory requirement for you to obtain indemnity insurance which will protect you in case you are sued. Nor are you required to be accredited or registered with any professional body. It is up to you whether you list these as operational requirements for your business but remember that both will cost you money and if they are not in your business plan you may forget to budget for them.

Data Protection Act 1998

The Data Protection Act 1998 does affect how you operate as a coach. The requirements of the Act are quite complicated and there is a guide for small businesses which you can access via the Information Commissioner's Office. A downloadable version is available on their website: www.informationcommissioner.gov. uk. The contact details are: helpline: 01625 545 745; email: mail@ico.qsi.gov.uk.

Any business that keeps client/customer details in electronic format and, under certain circumstances, on paper may be required to register with the Information Commissioner's Office. You are also required to ensure that personal information is:

- fairly and lawfully processed
- processed for specified purposes
- adequate, relevant and not excessive
- accurate and, where necessary, kept up to date
- not kept for longer than is necessary
- processed in line with the rights of the individual
- kept secure
- not transferred to countries outside the European Economic Area unless there is adequate protection for the information.

Not everyone needs to notify the Information Commissioner's Office. For example, if you are only processing and holding personal information (such as names, addresses, age) for core business purposes you may not need to notify. Examples of core business purposes include marketing, staff administration and accounting. This means that many coaching practices will not be required to register.

Check with the Information Commissioner's Office before making up your own mind as failure to notify when necessary is a criminal offence and you could be fined. The website includes an easy to understand form which you can work through online and provides you with the opportunity to notify online if required.

Equipment

Equipment is usually the main start-up cost for coaches as many start work from a home office. Once the absolute basics are covered, the most common equipment needs for the coach starting in business are:

- a reliable computer and printer
- a work station which meets health and safety needs
- a dedicated business phone line.

Financial forecasting and planning

Once you have described your proposed business you need to translate this information into figures which show how much it will cost to start-up and run your business and how much money the business will generate.

Information which you need before you can write this part of the plan includes:

- how much capital investment will be required to start the business (this is only needed if you are seeking investment from others)
- what security you will offer to lenders
- how you plan to pay back any money that you borrow
- what your sources of revenue will be.

Whether you are planning to become a sole trader or the CEO of a major new company providing coaching services, you are vital to the successful delivery of the plan. It will reassure investors if you put some information in here about your personal finances to show that you are clear about how you will survive the early and probably non-profit-making stages of growing the business.

When you are planning your finances you should forecast over the next three to five years. The bigger, more complex and ambitious your plans the more important it is to forecast well ahead. If you are seeking external financing for your business your financiers will want to understand how you intend to repay any loans or generate a good return on their investment. Detailed forecasts are often only possible for the first year, but don't let this stop you from trying as hard as you can to generate realistic longer-term forecasts. The more forethought you show you have put into planning your business the more seriously an investor will take your ideas. And remember, until you start working as a coach delivering your new coaching service your plan is just that – an idea for a business.

There is a lot of jargon you need to understand when you tackle this matter of describing and forecasting the financial aspects of your business. In the following list of information to include in your the financial forecasts I have tried to explain the terms simply enough for anyone to understand.

What are cash flow statements?

The movement of money into and out of your business is called 'cash flow'. Your business plan needs to show your prediction of the patterns of cash flow for your business. This is important. Businesses can go bust if they have to pay large bills (e.g. the wage bill) before customers pay for the goods or services they receive. If a business does not have enough money in the bank or access to credit to bridge this kind of gap then it may not survive its first year.

In your plan you should aim to show that your business will always have enough working capital to pay its way. This can be easy when you are a sole trader running a coaching service. You do not have to buy large quantities of supplies as a shopkeeper would and your clients should be paying as they go rather than racking up large bills. However, if you chose to coach for corporate clients and to employ other coaches to deliver this service, you might quickly find that slow payment of bills by your corporate clients when set against the requirement to pay your employees monthly creates a financial black hole.

You cannot change single-handedly the financial habits of large companies. Slow payers are the bane of small businesspeople. But you can plan for this eventuality and show in your forecasts that you know how you will handle this likely eventuality.

What is a profit and loss forecast?

This is the prediction of the total money you expect to bring into the business minus the costs of running the business.

Imagine that your rent, rates, wages bill and other costs are forecast to be £32,000 in Year 1. You plan to bring in £37,000 in fees in that year for coaching services.

What is your forecast going to be? A profit or a loss?

In this happy situation you will be forecasting a profit of £5,000.

Don't panic if you find yourself forecasting a loss for Year 1.

Building a viable business takes time. It is often the case that the time it takes to establish a business and market it successfully to clients leads to a loss-making first year.

The importance of a profit and loss forecast in your business plan is that it shows that you have predicted and planned for the outcomes shown.

What is a sales forecast?

This is the amount of money you expect to raise from sales. It is not the same as your profits as I hope was made clear in the previous paragraph.

A sales forecast provides the figures that anchor your marketing strategy in reality. Imagine if you described an extensive marketing drive in your business plan then showed very little growth in sales anywhere in your plan? People would wonder why you were bothering with the time or money costs of a vigorous marketing drive if the results could not be seen in your sales forecast.

The sales forecast is usually a month-by-month guide to predicted levels of sales. It is a vital tool which you need to keep updated throughout the life of your business. By setting goals for your sales you will be able to:

- track progress
- identify trends (e.g. lower demand for coaching at holiday times, higher demand in the New Year) and plan accordingly
- avoid cash flow problems by predicting income
- take early action to fix problems if real sales fall below predictions
- motivate yourself and others to keep on track.

Management

Most coaching businesses start with one person offering their coaching skills. If this is your intention then you might think that a section in your business plan about management is highly irrelevant. After all you won't require a management team, a board of directors or a clear structure for line management of staff.

However, you do need to think about the key tasks involved in managing a small business. Think about the following list of tasks:

- marketing (including website and other materials)
- finance
- administration
- developing your service
- monitoring the business.

This might be the point at which you realise that you do not have all the skills required to perform every task well. As always, you have a choice. For example, you could:

- decide to contract in some help
- decide to invest in further training.

Whatever you choose to do, having thought about it you will know if the actions you plan to take will be a cost to the business. If you have uncovered additional costs now is the time to go back and revise your financial plan.

Planning for risks

Coaching encourages optimism and there is every reason to focus on the positive. It isn't only sportspeople who feel they can influence the outcome of an important race through the power of positive thinking. Lots of successful business people feel that positive thinking has made a huge contribution to their success.

Positive thinking does not mean you have to ignore potential problems. An honest assessment of the risks you are taking in starting your business will ensure you are well-prepared if things do go wrong. Spotting potential risks gives you a chance to minimise them before you even start. For example:

- If you lack management experience then seek advice or recruit a mentor before you start.

- If you want to minimise the risk of bad debts then do what most coaches do – ask for full payment before you start work.

- Make sure your office equipment is insured against damage and loss.

- Provide for a contingency fund should the business take off more slowly than you have planned.

- If your target market is small, then be ready to broaden out and chase another if initial predictions for business growth prove to be inaccurate.

You are now in possession of all you need to know in order to write your business plan.

12

The Beginning is Not the End

Many times throughout this book I have used the term 'mentor' to describe someone who can inspire you, support you and shine the light of their experience on your business plans and challenges. Even if you already have a mentor for your coaching, consider finding a business mentor. Someone who understands the exciting challenges you will face as you move your business idea off the drawing board and into the real world.

A top quality mentor will help with one of the most important challenges you face when you start your own business: your development as a coach and businessperson. The world will not stand still while you focus on your business. To stay at the top of your game you need to:

- continue to hone your coaching skills through practice and other learning

- stay in touch with developments, trends and new ideas in the coaching world

- be aware of cultural and political trends which could create new coaching markets or opportunities

- be aware of policies, economic factors and legislation that affect business

- stay on top of the trends in your own business and take swift action to address matters such as a downturn in client numbers or increasing costs which threaten your business's viability.

I suspect this list of key responsibilities would be overwhelming if I extended it to include all your other responsibilities in life. There is nothing here about family, friends or your general physical and mental well-being. Have I made my point? You are going to need help throughout your business life. Never be too proud or too stubborn to seek it out.

CONTINUING PROFESSIONAL DEVELOPMENT

I feel very strongly that you owe it to yourself and to your clients to keep your skills up to speed and to keep continuously improving as a coach. You can choose to ignore this. After all, there is no governing body or legislation requiring you to attend courses in coaching. You can market yourself as a coach without acquiring any qualifications at all. I don't recommend this approach as a springboard to a successful business, but I do recognise the challenge of being torn between the demands of the day and investment in the future.

My best business decision

Maintaining a focus on my own development has been the key enabler of any progress I have made. My methods of study vary, e.g. books, training courses, seminars, writing a learning diary or getting coaching myself. This self-development forms the foundation of both my coaching ability and my commercial stability.

My biggest mistake
Julie declined to answer this one as she doesn't relate to any of her experiences as 'big mistakes'. Good positive attitude!

Julie Starr, Director, Starr Consulting, +44 (0) 845 125 9202, www.starrconsulting.co.uk

All continuing professional development is an investment in the future – your future. In coaching the lack of legislation means it is up to you to work out how to learn your coaching skills initially and how to keep them fresh. It may not stay this way. There have been interesting developments in the field of sports coaching in the UK that may well signal the likely trajectory of regulation in the fields of personal, executive and life coaching. In sports coaching the rules have been tightened in recent years. In order to become a licensed coach one must attend specific accredited courses. Each level of qualification carries with it certain levels of authorised activity. For example, a Level 1 coach can only coach under the supervision of a Level 2 coach. Insurance for clearly defined sports coaching activities is extended to all license holders free of charge but only if they coach within the terms of their license. As most sports coaching in the UK is conducted by volunteers, the regulations are implemented in a fairly light-touch manner. However, there is a requirement that coaches engage in specified levels of continuing professional development to maintain their license. There is a points-based system in operation and coaches must acquire a certain number of points per year by attending certain courses or carrying out a range of supervised and unsupervised activities and assignments as proof of continued learning.

My best business decision
Concentrating on providing a completely client-focused service delivered with passion, integrity, desire for client success and oodles of love.

My biggest mistake
At times, I've allowed the bullying and intimidation from the bully boy competitors to affect my business decision-making, instead of listening to my intuition and using my experience and knowledge.

Curly Martin, International Bestselling Author, Coach, Director. Achievement Specialists Ltd, www.achievement specialists.co.uk

My best business decision
Trusting my instincts and becoming a life coach after having worked for years as a research scientist for a think-tank.

My biggest mistake
It was with my first ever client when I tried to 'copy' another coach's method of working with people and work that way myself. It was disastrous. I felt incredibly stressed and was of very little help at all to my client. As soon as she left, I vowed never to do that again.

Sally Ann Law, M.A., Ph.D., Personal and Executive Life Coach, www.sally annlaw-lifecoach.co.uk

Nothing like this currently exists in your coaching world. There is no single recognised UK or European body with the authority to impose a similar system. It is also the case that the standard of coach training courses is wildly variable. Courses are fairly costly and it takes a major investment of research time, attendance time and money in fees to live up to a genuine commitment to develop your skills through attending courses.

This is not a reason for missing out on CPD. At the very least engaging in regular supervision and recording these sessions is a good step towards showing that you are engaged in reflecting and learning from your practice as a coach. You should also maintain a learning log. This can include:

■ a record of client coaching hours
■ a record of courses attended
■ a record of books and articles read
■ a record of any books or articles you publish on the subject of coaching
■ other information/evidence relating to your development as a coach.

The European Mentoring and Coaching Council (www.emccoun-cil.org) has been developing quality standards for coach education. Full details are available from its website. Other institutions are also taking on the challenge of setting recognised standards for coach training and development. For the time being we are likely to inhabit a world of competing systems. In this situation you should consider whose advice is likely to be the most highly valued by the gatekeepers to the types of clients you wish to coach.

For example, if you want to target corporate clients you should keep an eye on the advice of the Chartered Institute of Personnel and Development on matters relating to coach training and accreditation. This organisation is hugely influential in this field. You should also look at well-known institutions such as The Work Foundation (www.theworkfoundation.com). What they have to say about standards in coaching and how to assess/demonstrate competence in this field will influence employers.

Private clients will place their trust in well-known brands. Letters after your name are no guarantee of quality unless they were awarded by an institution they trust. If they can reassure themselves through knowing that your coaching qualifications

What the European Mentoring and Coaching Council says about its new quality standards for coach education:

The standards have been created from the basis of the extensive competency research conducted by EMCC in 2005 and 2006 but go much further than this to define the levels of practice, the contexts, reflection and planning as well as the theory.

Currently there are four categories of award – Foundation, Intermediate, Practitioner and Master. These are equivalent to the UK to NVQs levels 3 and 4 and 5 (undergraduate degree) and to postgraduate certificates, diplomas and master's degree.

The essence of this work is to provide a framework against which current or new programmes can be benchmarked and developed on the basis of equivalence.

www.emccouncil.org/eu/public/ european_quality_award/index.html and further learning took place under the supervision of an educational institution with a good general reputation, they will be more likely to choose you as their coach.

AND FINALLY...

Starting a business might seem like the hardest work you have done in your life but be prepared for a shock. The hardest part is yet to come. Once you have started your business you have to keep it going, week after week, year after year.

This requires motivation, stamina, intelligence and the ability to see the big picture. Just as one swallow doesn't make a summer, one bad week does not signal the end of your livelihood. You will have to be robust enough mentally and financially to ride out lean times, and energetic enough to cope with the boom times. Throughout it all you have to keep your eyes on longer-term goals and ensure that you are on track to reach them.

It is a tough job. Who better to take it on than you?

Useful Resources

This is a list of organisations and publications providing information and advice of value to people starting up a coaching business.

COACH LEARNING AND DEVELOPMENT

Listing and reviews of coaching courses:

Guardian Online: http://education.guardian.co.uk/courses/
Hotcourses website: www.hotcourses.com

Organisations offering training and information

Achievement Specialists: www.achievementspecialists.co.uk
Association for Professional Executive Coaching and Supervision: www.apecs.org/index.asp
Chartered Institute of Personnel and Development (CIPD): www.cipd.co.uk
The Coaching and Mentoring Network: www.coachingnetwork.org.uk
European Mentoring and Coaching Council: www.emccouncil.org
ICS Home Learning: www.icslearn.co.uk
International Association of Coaching: www.certifiedcoach.org
International Coach Federation: www.coachfederation.org.uk

USEFUL PUBLICATIONS

The Life Coaching Handbook, Curly Martin, Crown House Publishing, 2001.

Coaching for Performance, John Whitmore, Nicholas Brealey Publishing, 2003.

The Coaching Manual: The Definitive Guide to the Process and Skills of Personal Coaching, Julie Starr, Pearson, 2002.

BUSINESS KNOWLEDGE/SKILLS LEARNING AND DEVELOPMENT

Listing and reviews of business courses

Guardian Online: http://education.guardian.co.uk/courses

Hotcourses: www.hotcourses.com

Organisations offering business training and start-up information

ACAS: www.acas.org.uk

Business Gateway (Scotland): www.bgateway.com

Businesslink: www.businesslink.gov.uk

Department for Business Enterprise and Regulatory Reform: www.berr.gov.uk

European Federation of Black Women Business Owners: www.efbwbo.net

HM Revenue and Customs: www.hmrc.gov.uk

ICS: Home learning specialists: www.icslearn.co.uk

Learning at Home: www.learning-at-home.co.uk

Ready to Start – run by the charity Leonard Cheshire offering support to people with disabilities starting in business: www.readytostart.org.uk

Women in Business Network: www.wibn.co.uk

Women's Business Development Agency: www.wbda.co.uk

workSMART (backed by the TUC): www.worksmart.org.uk

Index